Marian Consecration

······ FOR ······

CHILDREN

Marian Consecration

FOR

CHILDREN

Bringing Mary to Life in Young Hearts and Minds

Carrie Gress

TAN Books
Gastonia, North Carolina

Cover and interior design by Caroline K. Green

Cover art: Mary with Child and Angels, right panel of Wilton Diptych, c.1395-9 (egg tempera on wood), Anonymous / National Gallery, London, UK / Bridgeman Images

ISBN: 978-1-5051-1118-7

Published in the United States by
TAN Books
PO Box 269
Gastonia, NC 28053
www.TANBooks.com

Printed and bound in India

FOR ALL THE CHILDREN OF THE WORLD,
BUT ESPECIALLY FOR MY GODCHILDREN

Simon Boldy

Sarah Miller

Renee Brown

Anne Gress

Aletheia Lovett

Grace Boldy

Theodore Church

Declan Carney

Miya Stibora

Contents

Part IV: Vices and Virtues

Part V: Knights and Princesses

A NOTE TO PARENTS

The idea for this book started a few years ago when I sought to find a suitable book for Marian consecration that I could read with my children. I assumed I would have a lot to choose from but was astounded to find very little. (I have since found a couple titles, but only after starting work on this project.) I asked a priest friend for a recommendation, and his quick reply was: "There isn't one. You should write it."

It took me awhile to become convinced that I really should write this book because, after all, I'm not a priest, religious, or a theologian. What business did I have writing a prayer book? But a year after this idea was hatched, I wrote *The Marian Option: God's Solution to a Civilization in Crisis*. It was a book that seemed to come to me out of the blue, and yet it was great preparation for this work. Not only did it require a crash course (or courses) on Mary and Mariology, it also opened my eyes to the basic need our world has for a greater devotion to Our Lady.

As I conducted my research on *The Marian Option*, something happened that I didn't anticipate: Mary became a real person. In discovering and writing about the many ways she assists us in the world, I began to see her not as some distant spiritual figure but as a doting mother who cares about the wellbeing of her children and will do everything within her power to protect us. It is my hope that this consecration will help your child see her as more real, more accessible, and as more of a mother than they previously knew. We may talk about her a lot, but do we really know her as a tender and loving mother who fiercely guards us, protects us, suffers for us, and intercedes for us?

A look around the world today can leave parents feeling helpless about how to prepare their children for an uncertain future. And yet there are few things that can prepare them better than a strong relationship with their spiritual Mother. Marian devotion is not limited to adults. History is full of child saints and children to whom Mary has appeared with special messages for the world. This is no accident. These children were chosen because of their deep humility and trust. Children have a special place in salvation history because of their docility and earnest love for God. Just because they're children does not mean that they are childish. Many child saints have displayed profound spiritual maturity, particularly in the face of great suffering and struggle.

Our children have a great capacity for spiritual growth, which can also serve as an example to us. Their fresh eyes can see God in the world in remarkable and beautiful ways. Today, many adults are blind when it comes to this type of vision, and yet our world needs it now more than ever. We need to see the roles that God and his mother play in our everyday lives.

We can sometimes forget the spiritual potential of children, but we must remember that our job is to help them come to know Jesus and his mother, because they cannot love what they do not know. Maria Montessori's approach recognized that the child's soul is asking for one thing: "Help me to come closer to God by myself." This is how a true relationship is fostered. We cannot force the relationship, but we can help lead the child to it so that there is a lasting bond. This book is an attempt to help children grasp and interiorize a strong devotion to Our Lady so that they can love her as the mother that she is and so that she can ultimately lead them to her Son, Mary's true mission.

In this book, I look at many different tales, stories, and Gospel readings, many of which your child might already be familiar with. Storytelling is a lost art in our world, and yet it is invaluable in forming the mental structures for moral living. Stories are what help cultures live on as one generation passes down to the next tales of bravery, courage, and moral ideals that form a community with a collective memory.

Beyond cultural importance, stories can also provide a sort of "short hand" for conveying a message. As adults, we're used to seeing references to stories, books, or movies that we are already familiar with and that drive home a message. I wanted to tap into this latent knowledge that children have from being read to (or from their own reading) in order to make learning about Mary a richer and more welcoming experience. Familiarity with what they already know helps do that.

While this book is written for reading children to use on their own, it could be a wonderful family project. As Fr. Peyton, the Rosary Priest, is famous for saying, "The family that prays together, stays together." All the more so for the family that unites itself together under the mantle of Our Lady, entrusting all that we have and all that we are to her maternal care.

I have included optional questions to foster discussion with your children about the daily reflections. Additionally, I wanted to make this consecration manageable for busy families, so the prayers are kept to a minimum. Feel free to supplement the prayers with your own family devotions, such as a nightly Rosary.

My prayer and hope is that this book will draw your children, and your whole family, closer to the Blessed Mother so that she can lead you home to her Son.

CHILDREN'S INTRODUCTION:
WHY CONSECRATE YOURSELF TO MARY?

"I'm scared," said Piglet. "A story will help," said Pooh. "How?" "Oh. Don't you know? Stories make your heart grow."

So just what is Marian consecration? Well, it's a practice that started long ago as a way to draw closer to Mary. When Jesus was on the cross, he gave Mary to John and John to Mary; this signified that Mary was to become the mother of all of humanity. She is our mother and we know that she longs to have a relationship with each of us. Marian consecration is making a gift of ourselves to the Queen of Heaven so that she may better be able to direct us, mother us, and love us in a way most pleasing to God.

In our world, it's easy to feel small, as if our little efforts account for nothing. But when we are united with Mary, she can take even our smallest offerings and make them useful in God's plan. When we consecrate ourselves to Mary, we bind ourselves to her even more closely as her spiritual children so that every effort, no matter how small, can be magnified by her love and become a proper gift to God.

Perhaps you already have a close relationship with Mary and know a lot about her. Or perhaps you don't. Either way, this book is going to help you understand her better as a real mother who knows and loves you and who wants to help you in your every need.

This consecration has thirty-three days of preparation following the adult versions of Marian consecration. Each day includes a short reflection, some questions to think about or discuss with your family, a short piece of Marian or Church trivia, and, finally, daily prayers.

The preparation is broken up into five parts. The first five days will focus on getting to know Jesus and his mother; after that, we will take a week to look at Mary as our mother. The third installment will tell the stories of young saints and their important role in salvation history, even in their littleness. Following this, we will consider the vices, or sins, that sadly separate us from Jesus and his mother, as well as the virtues that help bring us closer to them. Finally, the last week will look at what the stories of knights and princesses from the days of old can teach us about Mary and our own mission in the world. On the thirty-fourth day, you will then make the Act of Consecration, which is the gift of self to Our Lady through a prayer of consecration.

There are a lot of stories you will hear throughout these next thirty-three days. Some will be familiar and some may be new. But all of them will help you get to know Our Lady and your particular mission in life, even now as a young person.

CHOOSING YOUR MARIAN FEAST: WHEN TO START

Like other Marian consecrations, this one has thirty-three days of preparation broken up into different stages. Select a Marian feast day and then begin on the start date provided in the following table that corresponds with that feast.

The day chosen for consecration will become your feast day (or your child's) and will likely play an important role in your life. In my own life, I can see a clear pattern connected to the feast of my consecration, the feast of the Annunciation, March 25. The Annunciation has long been my favorite decade of the Rosary, and I love lilies, which are a symbol of this feast. I

MARIAN CONSECRATION FOR CHILDREN

was also married on March 25. Every person's mission is different, but it is beautiful when God reveals little clues about his will for our lives in these dates and feasts.

Start	Marian Feast	Consecration
Jan. 9	Apparition at Lourdes	Feb. 11
Feb. 20	The Annunciation	March 25★
April 10	Our Lady of Fatima	May 13
April 21	Mary, Help of Christians	May 24
April 28	The Visitation	May 31
May 25	Our Lady of Perpetual Help	June 27
June 13	Our Lady of Mt. Carmel	July 16
July 13	The Assumption	Aug. 15
July 20	Queenship of Mary	Aug. 22
Aug. 6	Nativity of the Virgin Mary	Sept. 8
Aug. 10	Holy Name of Mary	Sept. 12
Aug. 13	Our Lady of Sorrows	Sept. 15
Sept. 4	Our Lady of the Rosary	Oct. 7
Oct. 17	Our Lady of Divine Providence	Nov. 19
Oct. 19	Presentation of the Virgin Mary	Nov. 21
Oct. 25	Our Lady of the Miraculous Medal	Nov. 27
Nov. 5	Immaculate Conception	Dec. 8
Nov. 9	Our Lady of Guadalupe	Dec 12
Nov. 29	Mary, Mother of God	Jan. 1
Dec. 31	Presentation of Our Lord	Feb. 2

★If a leap year, start on February 21st.

Please note that some of these feasts can be moved if they fall on a Sunday, or Advent, or during the Easter Octave. It is worth looking at the liturgical calendar year to be sure before starting.

PART I

Jesus and His Mother

Jesus in *The Chronicles of Narnia*

It has been roughly two thousand years since Jesus walked the earth. During his time here, St. John says that Jesus did so many things that the world could not hold all the books it would take to tell his stories (see Jn 21:25). We hear a lot about Jesus at church during the Mass, but sometimes we forget how remarkable Jesus is. We're used to hearing about him walking on water, turning water into wine, and that he is Our Savior. But sometimes it's good to try to find a new way to see him; this can remind us of how much he loves us and how much he did for each of us.

In *The Chronicles of Narnia*, author C. S. Lewis offers a new way to look at Jesus through the character of Aslan, the great and powerful Lion. Lewis wrote seven books in the *Narnia* series, and Aslan is the only character who appears in all of them. In these books, Aslan creates, saves, gives hope, restores life, and cherishes the children and creatures of Narnia in much the same way we can imagine Christ doing with us. It shouldn't strike us as odd that Lewis would imagine Jesus as a lion. In the Bible, he is referred to as the Lion of Judah (see Rv 5:5).

We get a good look at Aslan in *The Magician's Nephew* when young Polly and Digory access a new world through magical golden rings. They witness Aslan creating Narnia and filling it with all sorts of creatures, great and small, who can talk, including mice, dwarves, fauns, and centaurs (half man, half horse). After creating this new world, Aslan then appoints a king and queen, bringing order to this new world. In a funny twist, the first royal couple was a taxi cab driver and his wife, who had been hanging laundry when they were thrust into this new land. They were hardly noble but some-how rose to the occasion.

Lewis includes many humanizing details that help us feel close to Aslan, like a sense of humor, happiness, and compassion (which we will talk more about on Day 3). But we also get a sense of Aslan's strength and power. "Aslan threw up his shaggy head, opened his mouth, and uttered a long, single note; not very loud, but full of power. Polly's heart jumped in her body when she heard it. She felt sure that it was a call, and that anyone who heard that call would want to obey it." Aslan, like Jesus, is all-good, so when we hear his divine voice, we get a sense that it is important we should follow it.

In *The Lion, the Witch, and the Wardrobe,* Lewis makes it clear that Aslan is both wonderful and terrifying—but terrifying in a good way because he is so powerful beyond our experience. "People who have not been to Narnia sometimes think that a thing cannot be good and terrible at the same time. If the children had ever thought so, they were cured of it now. For when they tried to look at Aslan's face they just caught a glimpse of the golden mane and the great, royal, solemn, overwhelming eyes; and then found they couldn't look at him and went all trembly."

Jesus, like Aslan, can make us feel "trembly," but he is also all-loving. The more we come to know him in our minds and hearts, the more we will want to follow him.

Discussion Questions

1. How do you think you can feel both terror and wonder for the same thing, like the children felt when they met Aslan?

2. What do you imagine Jesus will be like?

3. Do you think a story about a lion like Aslan in *The Chronicles of Narnia* helps you understand Jesus better? If so, in what ways?

Did You Know?

C. S. Lewis used a lion to represent Jesus because there is an old title that refers to him as the Lion of Judah. One of the ancient Jewish tribes was called Judah and their symbol was a lion. This image was used in the New Testament in the Book of Revelation where it speaks of a man who had a vision of a scroll, and he was looking to find someone worthy to open it. No man in heaven, on earth, or under the earth, was able to open it. The man says, "I shed many tears because no one was found worthy to open the scroll or to examine it. One of the elders said to me, 'Do not weep. The lion of the tribe of Judah, the root of David, has triumphed, enabling him to open the scroll'" (Rv 5:4–5). This lion of the tribe of Judah is Jesus, the word of God, who is able to open the scroll.

Prayers for the Day

Our Father

Our Father,
who art in heaven,
hallowed be thy name;
thy kingdom come,
thy will be done,
on earth as it is in heaven.
Give us this day our daily bread,
and forgive us our trespasses,
as we forgive those who trespass against us;
and lead us not into temptation,
but deliver us from evil.
Amen.

Hail Mary

Hail Mary, full of grace,
the Lord is with thee.
Blessed are thou among women,
and blessed is the fruit of thy womb, Jesus.

Holy Mary, Mother of God,
pray for us sinners now,
and at the hour of our death.
Amen.

Aslan and the Stone Table

I n *The Lion, the Witch, and the Wardrobe,* Peter, Susan, Edmund, and Lucy Pevensie are the nephews and nieces of Digory, who we mentioned on Day 1. The Pevensie children go to live with their Uncle Digory during World War II to escape the German bombs that are being dropped on London. On a rainy day, during a thrilling game of hide-and-go-seek, Lucy happens upon a wardrobe. Sliding through old fur coats, she quickly discovers the wardrobe has no back, and she finds herself in the wintery forest of Narnia with a faun named Mr. Tumnus. After enjoying cakes, tea, and stories with Mr. Tumnus, the faun urges Lucy to return to her family because of the White Witch.

Later, Lucy leads all the children back into Narnia through the old wardrobe. While there, her brother Edmund happens to encounter the White Witch. Angry with his older brother, Peter, and lured by the magical Turkish Delight candy and a promise to be a king, Edmund betrays his siblings and all the good creatures in Narnia by siding with the witch. After he reveals to the witch the whereabouts of his siblings and their planned meeting place with Aslan, he realizes that she has tricked him. Not only will she not make him a king or give him Turkish Delight, but she begins to treat him terribly since she now knows where to find the others. Through his betrayal, Edmund becomes the witch's slave, and he suffers greatly not only from her physical abuse but also because of the awareness of his betrayal.

The witch, her goons, and Edmund race to the Stone Table where they know the other Pevensies and Aslan will be. But as they travel there in a sledge made for snow, the cold starts to thaw and spring arrives. They must continue on foot, but at a much slower pace. Edmund is whipped, fed scraps of stale bread, and not allowed to rest as the group trudges toward the Stone Table.

Eventually, Edmund and his family are reunited, and he expresses how very sorry he is for betraying them. But the White Witch still has a claim upon his soul because of his sin. Aslan, then, must offer himself to go in Edmund's place. In the middle of the night, the White Witch and other cruel and vicious creatures kill Aslan at the Stone Table. Only Lucy and Susan witness it all.

The Stone Table is a symbol of Jesus's cross and the offer he made of himself, an offer that freed us from the bonds of the devil. Some of the details are changed because it is not possible to crucify a lion, but even in later stories, we get a sense of the importance of Aslan's sacrificial gift to Edmund because the Stone Table continues to be honored.

Discussion Questions

1. Why do you think C. S. Lewis used a table for the death of Aslan?

2. What was it that made Edmund betray his family? And what was it that made him return?

3. In what ways does Aslan's sacrifice for Edmund look like Jesus's sacrifice for us?

Did You Know?

The true cross of Jesus was said to be found by St. Helena, the queen mother of Emperor Constantine, on her journey to the Holy Land. She went to Calvary and found three crosses. Unsure which was the true cross of Christ, she asked that a very sick young girl who was near death be brought to the place where the crosses were. When the first cross was carried over to the fading girl, she showed no signs of improvement. The same thing happened with the second. But when the third cross was brought close to her, the girl's fever broke and she asked for something to eat. She was healed! Everyone knew this was the true cross of Christ.

Prayers for the Day

Our Father

Our Father,
who art in heaven,
hallowed be thy name;
thy kingdom come,
thy will be done,
on earth as it is in heaven.
Give us this day our daily bread,
and forgive us our trespasses,
as we forgive those who trespass against us;
and lead us not into temptation,
but deliver us from evil.
Amen.

Hail Mary

Hail Mary, full of grace,
the Lord is with thee.
Blessed are thou among women,
and blessed is the fruit of thy womb, Jesus.

Holy Mary, Mother of God,
pray for us sinners now,
and at the hour of our death.
Amen.

DAY 3
....

The Tears of Jesus

In *The Magician's Nephew,* Digory's mother is very sick and may soon die. Although Digory has done something he is ashamed of, something he knows Aslan would not like, he overcomes his shame and approaches the great lion for help. "But please, please—won't you—can't you give me something that will cure Mother?" Digory asks. And then something unexpected happened:

> Up until then he had been looking at the Lion's great feet and the huge claws on them; now, in his despair, he looked up at its face. What he saw surprised him as much as anything in his whole life. For the tawny face was bent down near his own and (wonder of wonders) great shining tears stood in the Lion's eyes. They were such big, bright tears compared with Digory's own that for a moment he felt as if the Lion must really be sorrier about his Mother than he was himself.

The shortest passage in the English Scripture is "And Jesus wept" (Jn 11:35). The tears were for his friend Lazarus who had died. Jesus's compassion and suffering with us did not end when his life ended. He still feels intense pain, suffering with us—perhaps even more so than we do—just like Digory saw in the eyes of Aslan, who was like Jesus in his tears.

Digory knows that apples from a particular tree in Narnia have the power to heal. He confesses to Aslan that he wanted to steal an apple and give it to his mother directly, because he wasn't sure if Aslan would give him one. This should remind us of the fruit that Adam and Eve stole and ate from the tree in the Garden of Eden, even though God forbid them to do so. Aslan tells the boy that, yes, his mother would have been healed, but because the healing did not come in the right way—because it was taken without permission—it would only cause more pain for Digory and his mother. It would have ruined their relationship. "Understand, then," Aslan explains, "that it would have healed her; but not to your joy or hers. The day would have come when both you and she would have looked back and said it would have been better to die in that illness." Today, we wish that Eve and Adam didn't eat the forbidden fruit because of the many bad things that it led to for the rest of us.

Meanwhile, Digory is still left wondering what will happen to his mother.

"That is what *would* have happened, child, with a stolen apple," Aslan continued. "It is not what will happen now. What I give you now will bring joy. It will not, in your world, give endless life, but it will heal. Go. Pluck her an apple from the Tree."

Immediately thereafter, Digory makes his way back home with the healing apple, cuts it up for his mother, and just as Aslan had promised, she is restored to health.

Jesus cares about us, and he understands both how we have been created and the rest of nature. This is why he has given us so many wise rules to help us order our lives; he knows these rules will help us experience joy by doing things the right way instead of pain and sorrow when we do them the wrong way.

Discussion Questions

1. Why does Aslan say that an apple taken from the magic tree without permission would still have healed Digory's mother?

2. Why wouldn't this have made Digory and his mother happy though?

3. Why is it important to do things in the right way and at the right time?

Did You Know?

There are several plants called the Tears of Jesus, or Christ's Tear. The Tears of Jesus plant is also known as the wax plant because its flowers look like they are made out of wax. The waxy flowers ooze a sweet nectar that drops upon the leaves and looks like tears. One species of the plant only blooms every seven years!

Prayers for the Day

Our Father

Our Father,
who art in heaven,
hallowed be thy name;
thy kingdom come,
thy will be done,
on earth as it is in heaven.
Give us this day our daily bread,
and forgive us our trespasses,
as we forgive those who trespass against us;
and lead us not into temptation,
but deliver us from evil.
Amen.

Hail Mary

Hail Mary, full of grace,
the Lord is with thee.
Blessed are thou among women,
and blessed is the fruit of thy womb, Jesus.

Holy Mary, Mother of God,
pray for us sinners now,
and at the hour of our death.
Amen.

Mary Is God's Masterpiece

Many artists have a work they are most proud of called a "masterpiece." They work very hard to create it after spending years trying to perfect their skills. Most don't even attempt such a project until they feel their skills are up to the task of making their best piece. God is like an artist when he creates. And the most perfect being that he created, over all the angels and saints, is Our Lady.

Yes, God made all of creation and he "found it very good" (Gn 1:31). But if all of creation was good, Mary is better. Some have speculated that Mary looked similar to Eve, but their responses to God couldn't have been more different. Instead of introducing sin into the world through her disobedience like Eve—saying "no" to God—Mary brought obedience to the world through her "yes" that she gave to the angel Gabriel. Mary was also created by God without sin, which is what the words *Immaculate Conception* mean. She was created in the womb of Saint Anne without any sin on her soul. She was and remains "full of grace."

Mary was a simple Jewish girl with few recorded words in the Bible. She wasn't famous and her family did not have a lot of money. Even though some might see these as weaknesses, God was able to show his great strength and might through her humble life.

In the Gospel of Luke, we learn of the meeting between Mary and the angel Gabriel. The beautiful angel greets her, "Hail Mary, full of grace, the Lord is with thee." Do these words sound familiar to you? They should, because they're the beginning of the *Hail Mary* prayer. The word *hail* is a

greeting, like saying "hello," except it is generally used to greet people of a special status, like a king or queen. So when we say "Hail Mary," we are basically saying hello to our queen!

After Mary agrees to be Jesus's mother, she goes to visit her cousin and friend, Elizabeth, who is pregnant with John the Baptist. When she arrives, Elizabeth utters the next lines from the *Hail Mary* prayer: "Blessed are thou among women, and blessed is the fruit of thy womb!" Mary then replies with a prayer of her own, now known as the Canticle of Mary, the Song of Mary, or the Magnificat:

> My soul proclaims the greatness of the Lord; my spirit rejoices in God my savior. For he has looked upon his handmaid's lowliness; behold, from now on will all ages call me blessed. The Mighty One has done great things for me, and holy is his name. (Lk 1:46–49)

Even though Mary admits she is a lowly handmaid, she has indeed been called "blessed" by all generations. We know her today as the most powerful woman in history. No woman has been painted more, had more songs written about her, or changed the outcome of battles that appeared to be lost. The only explanation for this is that she is the masterpiece of God. He created her perfect and without any sin on her soul.

Discussion Questions

1. Have you ever made something that you were very proud of?

2. What do you think a perfect mother would look like?

3. How do you think it made God feel when Mary said yes to his plans?

Did You Know?

The tabernacle is the gold box at church where the Eucharist—that is, the consecrated Host—is placed when there is some left over after communion. The idea of a tabernacle has a long history that dates back to the Book of Exodus when the Jews escaped the slavery of the Egyptians. During their forty years roaming through the desert, they carried with them a tabernacle called the Ark of the Covenant that was the earthly dwelling place of God. Tabernacles today, that house Christ in our churches, are named after the Israelite model. Mary is also considered Christ's first tabernacle and is also referred to as the New Ark of the Covenant because she held Jesus in her womb for nine months before his birth.

Prayers for the Day

Our Father

Our Father,
who art in heaven,
hallowed be thy name;
thy kingdom come,
thy will be done,
on earth as it is in heaven.
Give us this day our daily bread,
and forgive us our trespasses,
as we forgive those who trespass against us;
and lead us not into temptation,
but deliver us from evil.
Amen.

Hail Mary

Hail Mary, full of grace,
the Lord is with thee.
Blessed are thou among women,
and blessed is the fruit of thy womb, Jesus.

Holy Mary, Mother of God,
pray for us sinners now,
and at the hour of our death.
Amen.

Jesus and His Mother

Jesus and his mother are very close. He knows that it was Our Lady saying "yes" to the archangel Gabriel at the Annunciation that brought him into our world. Often, people think we don't need Mary as our mother, but she was obviously a very integral part of God's plan and so was essential to the story and to our salvation. If God found her so important, it stands to reason we should as well. Perhaps we can see this better if we look at the life of a mother and son in a different kind of story.

In the classic children's story *Little Lord Fauntleroy* by Frances Hodgson Burnett, an eight-year-old boy, Cedric Errol, discovers that his life as a happy American kid in New York City is about to take a dramatic change. Cedric's father died when he was just a year or two old, and he and his mother thought they had no other family in the world. But as it turned out, Cedric's father was the son of an earl from England. With all the other heirs to the family title and fortune dead, Cedric was the only heir left to inherit the vast lands, fortune, and responsibility. His new title was to be Lord Fauntleroy until he, too, became the earl.

But Cedric's grandfather, the Earl of Dorincourt, was a greedy and selfish man and distrustful of many people. He also hated Cedric's mother because she was an American who had no fortune. The earl believed that she had only married Cedric's father because he was rich. So, when Cedric and his mother moved to England, his mother was not welcome to live with them but had to live alone at a house somewhere on the earl's great estate, far away from Cedric. She knew that it would be best for Cedric to be close to his grandfather and learn from him how to govern the vast estate. She sadly lived apart from her son, who meant every-thing in the world to her.

As the story continues, however, the Earl of Dorincourt is slowly affected by the new Lord Fauntleroy, who is good and generous, and the old man starts to do good things for those around him. The story ends when the earl realizes that he has been dramatically changed by his grandson from a mean, selfish man to a new man with a loving heart. He then realizes that Cedric is the child that he is because of who his mother is. Without such a wonderful mother, he would never have been such a wonderful son.

Many people want to cut Mary out of the life of Jesus, just like the earl wanted to remove Cedric's mother from his life. Without her, there would be no him. We also know that Mary was a very good mother. She was there for her son through his whole life and stayed near him during his passion and death. It must have been terrible for her to watch her son go through what he did for us.

Like a good son, or the perfect son, Jesus loves his mother so much because he knows that it was her openness to life that brought him into our world. It makes perfect sense, then, to consider that since he came to us through his mother, perhaps we should go back to him through his mother. As St. Louis de Montfort said, "There is no surer or easier way than Mary in uniting all men with Christ."

Discussion Questions

1. What do moms do to help their children become good people?

2. Imagine a world without good mothers. What do you think it would be like?

3. Why do you think Jesus loves his mother so much?

Did You Know?

Inside Notre Dame Cathedral at Chartres, France, is a silk relic of the veil that Mary is said to have worn when Jesus was born. It was given to the cathedral in 876 by the emperor Charlemagne. In 1145, the church burned down. Miraculously, several priests grabbed the veil and hid from the fire down in the crypt. Although they should have died from smoke inhalation, falling material, or the heat, the priests and the veil came out of the crypt three days later. Their survival was declared a miracle by a representative of the pope. You can still see this holy relic in the glorious gothic church built for Our Lady.

Prayers for the Day

Our Father

Our Father,
who art in heaven,
hallowed be thy name;
thy kingdom come,
thy will be done,
on earth as it is in heaven.
Give us this day our daily bread,
and forgive us our trespasses,
as we forgive those who trespass against us;
and lead us not into temptation,
but deliver us from evil.
Amen.

Hail Mary

Hail Mary, full of grace,
the Lord is with thee.
Blessed are thou among women,
and blessed is the fruit of thy womb, Jesus.

Holy Mary, Mother of God,
pray for us sinners now,
and at the hour of our death.
Amen.

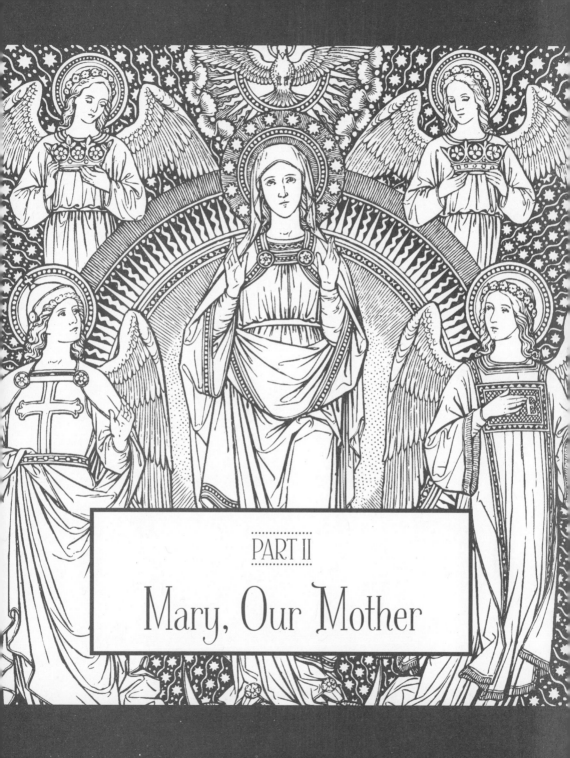

PART II

Mary, Our Mother

Mary Is Our Mother

One of Jesus's last statements that he made from the cross was to give his mother to the care of St. John, and St. John to the care of his mother. In this, Jesus was providing for the practical needs of the two people on earth who loved him the most, as witnessed by their willingness to follow him all the way up Calvary. But Jesus was doing more than that. He was also symbolically giving his mother to all humans. St. John represented all of us that day there on Mount Calvary when Jesus gave up his life for our sins. Mary isn't just the mother of Jesus, but she is *our* mother too.

We generally have a pretty good idea of what makes a good mother. We have lots of examples in books, especially Caroline Ingalls in *The Little House on the Prairie* books, Susan Sowerby in *The Secret Garden,* or even Marilla, Anne Shirley's adoptive mother in *Anne of Green Gables.* As someone once said of Mrs. Ingalls, "Ma represented the eternal, the things that cannot be taken away, and the life lessons that are more important than any amount of money."

But God has offered us a mother that is his masterpiece, and therefore, she is a perfect mother. And this perfect mother is *our* mother. She wants to help in every way that we can possibly imagine.

One of the things that mothers love best is staying close to their children. Even when children are far away, mothers are close to them in their thoughts and hearts. Mothers consider their children's every need and try to address all of their difficulties. This is also what Mary does. She knows you better than you know yourself, and she wants everything in your life to go according the will of God. She also knows what it cost Jesus to die on the cross for us, so she doesn't want to see that wasted or for us to throw it away as if it has no meaning.

Perhaps when you were very small, one of your parents, grandparents, or a teacher read you the book *The Runaway Bunny*. In the story, there is a little bunny who says that he is going to run away. But his mother says, "If you run away, I will run after you. For you are my little bunny." Then he threatens to become a fish in a trout stream, swimming away from his momma. And she says, "If you become a fish in a trout stream, I will become a fisherman and I will fish for you." This goes on with the little bunny threatening to become a rock on a mountain, a crocus in a hidden garden, a bird that flies away, a sailboat that sails away, and on and on. And to every one of the little bunny's threats to run away, momma bunny explains how she will follow after him and recover him.

If you become a rock, "I will become a mountain climber; and I will climb to where you are."

"If you become a crocus in a hidden garden, I will be a gardener and I will find you."

"If you become a bird and fly away from me, I will be a tree that you can come home to."

And so on. Finally, knowing his mother will find him no matter what he does, he decides that he should just remain where he is and stay his momma's little bunny.

Truly, this is the desire of every earthly mother, and also the desire of our heavenly Mother. There is no place that we can go beyond her reach. She will always do what she can to draw us back to herself and to her Son.

Discussion Questions

1. If Mary is a good mother (which we know she is), how do you think she wants to help you?

2. Can you think of things you might ask Mary to help you with?

3. Mary was always with Jesus, even as he went to die on the cross. Do you think she was like the bunny mom in the story *The Runaway Bunny*? How so?

Did You Know?

Mary has provided many messages and material tools to help us get to know her so we can trust her as our mother. These tools include the Brown Scapular that she presented to St. Simon Stock, which carries the promise that those who die while wearing it will go to heaven. Or the Miraculous Medal that Our Lady gave to St. Catherine Labouré, which features an image of her with her arms outstretched, as if waiting to embrace us. She has also appeared to many men, women, and children to pass along important messages and to encourage us all to pray and offer sacrifices for the world, especially for sinners.

Prayers for the Day

Earliest Known Prayer to Mary

Beneath your compassion,
we take refuge, O Mother of God:
do not despise our petitions in time of trouble:
but rescue us from dangers.
Amen.

Hail Mary

Hail Mary, full of grace,
the Lord is with thee.
Blessed are thou among women,
and blessed is the fruit of thy womb, Jesus.

Holy Mary, Mother of God,
pray for us sinners now,
and at the hour of our death.
Amen.

Mary Intercedes for Us

There is a very old story about a good and powerful king retold in the book *Take It to the Queen: A Tale of Hope,* written by Josephine Nobisso and beautifully illustrated by Katalin Szegedi.

The story starts with a beautiful village where most of the people live with many good things, such as fresh water, abundant crops, healthy horses, and strong bridges and homes. The king eventually chooses a queen from among the people. She is kind, good, and beautiful. The king sees that his queen has many virtues and shares his will to serve the people, especially the poorest and neediest, so he can refuse none of her requests.

Things go well for a time, but eventually the people grow tired of doing their work to maintain the village and forget the many blessings they receive from the king. Their obedience to him begins to lessen and they stop respecting him. When the king and queen one day have a son, he, too, is treated terribly because the people's hearts have grown cold. In fact, the people have such hard hearts that they kill the prince, not wanting him to be the king's heir.

In time, the people begin to suffer because of their rebellion. They lack food and clean water, and their village begins to crumble. They finally realize how terrible they have been but are too ashamed to ask the king for help since they had killed his son. Then the people remember their queen, who is tender and forgiving, and who was once one of them. Could she beg for the king's mercy? They hoped so.

Wanting to make amends with the king, they go to the queen for help.

They give her all that they have—a meager apple—to present it to the king as an offering of their sorrow for having hurt him so terribly.

The queen takes their humble offering, cuts it up, and gives it to the king. Though the gift was something very small, he cherished it because it came from his queen. This small offering was enough to restore the relationship between the king and the villagers. Their village once again became a beautiful place where people had clean water and plenty of food and livestock. The townsfolk knew they owed the queen much for helping to rescue them from their misery and restore their relationship with the king.

In another version of this story, told in St. Louis de Montfort's work on Mary, the queen is given bruised apples by the people. She cuts them up and makes them look much more pleasing than they were. She then gives the apples to the king, who enjoys them. He would certainly not have liked the offering had they shown up as damaged apples. Mary is that queen who takes our little offerings that are mixed with rot, bruises, and other imperfections and presents them anew to Our Lord. She knows that even though it was our sins that her son died for, she doesn't want his sacrifice to be wasted, so she does what she can to help us repair our relationship with the king—Our Father in heaven.

The queen in these stories could be called an "intercessor." This is someone who intervenes between two others, someone who comes between them and helps them make up after a conflict. We say that Mary is our intercessor, or that she intercedes for us.

Mary was chosen as a human to bring God in the form of Jesus to us. He was her son, and yet it was our sins that led to his death. And even though she knows of our guilt, she also knows that she is our mother and must help us to return to Jesus. The apples represent the humble offerings we make in prayers or sacrifices to him. She can present them to her Son and make them much better than they would be had we not asked for her help (she intercedes and makes the gift more pleasing). Even in our great weakness and littleness, anything that we give to Mary can be turned into something magnificent for God.

Discussion Questions

1. Why was the king open to listening to the queen when she made a request for the wretched people?

2. Who do you think the people, the queen, the king, and the prince represent in this tale?

3. Why do you think Mary is willing to intercede for people on earth?

Did You Know?

St. Louis Marie de Montfort is the saint who popularized Marian conse-cration. He wrote a book called *True Devotion to Mary*, and he predicted "that raging beasts will come with their teeth to gnarl and tear at this little book of mine or at least it will be buried in a coffer and forgotten." Just as he prophesized, the little book was lost for nearly one hundred years before being discovered in 1842 by a member of his order, the Sulpicians, who recognized the handwriting. It was published shortly thereafter. Since then, countless numbers of people have consecrated themselves to Mary.

Prayers for the Day

Earliest Known Prayer to Mary

Beneath your compassion,
we take refuge, O Mother of God:
do not despise our petitions in time of trouble:
but rescue us from dangers.
Amen.

Hail Mary

Hail Mary, full of grace,
the Lord is with thee.
Blessed are thou among women,
and blessed is the fruit of thy womb, Jesus.

Holy Mary, Mother of God,
pray for us sinners now,
and at the hour of our death.
Amen.

DAY 8

Mary Suffers With Us
and Wants to Heal Us

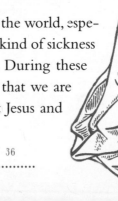

o one likes to suffer, but sometimes suffering is okay when we know it helps someone else. Perhaps you have given up a favorite toy to a sibling or friend because you knew that giving it to them would make them very happy. And while it may have been difficult to give up the toy, you were happy to make someone you love happy, so it was worth the pain. Or maybe you had a sore throat, and rather than complaining about it, you still helped your mother clean the kitchen because you knew she needed your help.

These are small glimpses into how Jesus and Mary understand suffering. Jesus offered himself for us on the cross. It is said that his worst suffering was the knowledge he had about the many souls who would reject his gift.

Often, we can feel very alone in the world, especially if we are suffering from some kind of sickness or something that hurts our heart. During these times, it is important to remember that we are not alone in our suffering and that Jesus and

Mary want to be close to us always, but especially during those times.

Given her maternal heart, Mary is very close to us in our suffering, just as she was with Jesus. She was with him during every step, fall, lashing, and indignity that he suffered in his passion. Some saints have speculated that she actually felt these pains in her body and that only through a special grace from God did she not die from the pain. Whether she felt Christ's pains or not, she knows how much Jesus suffered to free us from Satan's grip. She does not want to see Jesus's sufferings go to waste by us refusing the gift he made on the cross.

In *The Christmas Miracle of Jonathan Toomey* there are three sets of mothers and sons that deal with a lot of suffering and pain. Jonathan Toomey, referred to by many as Mr. Gloomy, is a grumpy woodcarver. What people don't know, though, is that he is so terribly sad because his wife and infant son died within three days of each other before he moved to the new town.

Widow McDowell and her son Thomas have just moved to town. During their move, they lost their nativity set. The widow hears that Mr. Toomey is the best woodworker around, so she asks him to carve her a new set in time for Christmas. "Pish-posh!" is Mr. Toomey's general response to Christmas, miracles, and the like. But he agrees to make the nativity set, saying it will be done when it is done, Christmas or not.

The widow and her seven-year-old son start to visit the woodshop so Thomas can watch Mr. Toomey work. Widow McDowell promises they will be quiet and sits down by the fire to knit. As the wood is cut, Thomas suggests that the sheep, although the most beautiful sheep he has ever seen, don't look right. His sheep from the old nativity set looked happy because they were in the presence of the baby Jesus. "Pish-Posh!" is Toomey's response. "Sheep are sheep. They cannot look happy."

And so it goes: Mr. Toomey carves, the widow knits, and Thomas adds his suggestions until all the pieces are almost finished, except for Mary and the baby Jesus. "I am about to begin the last two figures—Mary and the baby. Can you tell me how your figures looked?" Mr. Toomey asks. "They are the most special of all," Thomas explains. "Jesus was smiling and reaching up to his mother, and Mary looked like she loved him very much."

By Christmas Eve, Mr. Toomey had drawn many drafts of what he wanted the mother and child to look like, but he tossed them all into the fire because they were not quite right. Finally, he goes to a drawer and pulls out a sketch of his wife holding their son. The tears stream down his face as he looks at his deceased wife and child, but he knows they are the right inspiration for the Madonna and Child and goes about carving the last piece. The next day, as if a new man, Mr. Toomey presents the beautiful nativity set to Widow McDowell and Thomas. He joins them for church, and no one ever called him Mr. Gloomy again.

Mr. Toomey needed help to heal from his broken heart over the loss of his wife and son. Through the kind and Mary-like Widow McDowell and her Christ-like son, Thomas, great healing was brought to the sad wood-carver. But ultimately, the healing would not have happened without the Mother of God and her Son.

Discussion Questions

1. Mary suffered greatly when she watched her son die on the cross. Why was she willing to undergo this deep pain?

2. Do you think Mary suffers when she watches us, her spiritual children, suffer?

3. How did carving the Madonna and Child for the nativity set help Mr. Toomey?

Did You Know?

Nativity scenes are common to see around Christmastime. In Rome and many churches around the world, local parishes set up elaborate nativity scenes that include villages, barns, livestock, and towns people, all centered around the pivotal moment in history when Christ was born. The nativity scene, although dating back to Jesus's birth, was not found in the early church. The tradition wasn't widespread until 1223 when St. Francis of Assisi set up a nativity scene in Italy. He was inspired by a visit to the Holy Land when he saw the actual place where Christ was born. He wanted to bring that experience of worshipping the Christ Child to the people of Assisi. The faithful loved the idea and it has spread far and wide, even down to us today and the nativity scenes that we see at home or in our own church.

Prayers for the Day

Earliest Known Prayer to Mary

Beneath your compassion,
we take refuge, O Mother of God:
do not despise our petitions in time of trouble:
but rescue us from dangers.
Amen.

Hail Mary

Hail Mary, full of grace,
the Lord is with thee.
Blessed are thou among women,
and blessed is the fruit of thy womb, Jesus.

Holy Mary, Mother of God,
pray for us sinners now,
and at the hour of our death.
Amen.

We Cannot Give Mary Too Much

Sometimes people worry that they can love Mary too much. But no amount of our love could be more than the love Jesus shows his mother because he loves her with an infinite amount of love. So long as we are not making Mary into something she is not, like a goddess, then we cannot love her too much.

Imagine thinking you loved your parents too much. This is usually not something we worry about. We usually worry about *not* loving the people in our lives enough since we are human and prone to sin and selfishness. St. Maximillian Kolbe, who was very devoted to Our Lady, once said, "Never be afraid of loving the Blessed Virgin too much. You can never love her more than Jesus did."

Sometimes when people think about Marian consecration, they wonder what they will get out of it in return. The short answer is that we can never be outdone in generosity. Whatever we give or offer up to Our Lady, she will be even more generous with us. Because she is greater than we are, she is able to give us more.

The question seems to be answered best by looking at the classic book *Guess How Much I Love You.* You might be too old to enjoy this book anymore since it is for small children, but its message is still great for understanding how our love can never be outdone in generosity.

In the story, it is time for Little Nut Brown Hare to go to sleep, and he is trying to tell Big Nut Brown Hare how much he loves him. Little Nut Brown Hare thinks of the biggest things he can wrap his mind around, such as, "I love you as high as I can reach," and "I love you as high as I can hop," and "I love you all the way down the lane as far as the river."

But no matter what Little Nut Brown Hare suggests, Big Nut Brown Hare has an even better or bigger response; for example, he can reach and hop much higher than Little Nut Brown Hare. Finally, Little Nut Brown Hare thinks he has come up with the best response ever. He tells Big Nut Brown Hare, "I love you to the Moon." We all know that Big Nut Brown Hare was yet again able to come up with an even better response, "I love you to the Moon . . . and back."

This is how Our Lady works. She will always outdo any sort of idea or gift that we may be able to come up with, simply because of who she is and who we are. As God's masterpiece, her heart and mind are united to the Trinity, so she always knows how to outdo us in generosity. She is that mother who can honestly say, "I love you to the moon and back," or perhaps even better, "I love you to heaven and back."

Discussion Questions

1. Have you ever worried that you loved one of your family members too much?

2. Have you ever worried that perhaps you might not love someone enough, meaning that you didn't give them what they deserved, such as goodness and kindness?

3. Mary is always very generous with us, but sometimes in hidden ways. What ways do you think she might give us good things when we don't usually realize it?

Did You Know?

The moon is a common symbol of Mary because the moon reflects the light of the sun in a similar way that Mary reflects the light of her Son. St. Jacinta used to call it Mary's lantern. Just as the moon shows and tempers the sun's majesty to us in the darkness of the night, Mary can show us the light of her Son in a soft way that draws us back to him. Some also say that as the earth revolves around the sun and the moon around the earth, so our lives should revolve around Christ, but Mary is that doting mother who always hovers over us and watches after us.

Prayers for the Day

Earliest Known Prayer to Mary

Beneath your compassion,
we take refuge, O Mother of God:
do not despise our petitions in time of trouble:
but rescue us from dangers.
Amen.

Hail Mary

Hail Mary, full of grace,
the Lord is with thee.
Blessed are thou among women,
and blessed is the fruit of thy womb, Jesus.

Holy Mary, Mother of God,
pray for us sinners now,
and at the hour of our death.
Amen.

Mary Is a Warrior

Most people think of Mary as little more than a beautiful figure who can inspire beautiful art, or even as just someone who is very sweet but not very helpful when it comes to the real world. If we look to history, though, we can see that Mary has done a great many things to help Christians. She has helped them reclaim their lands from Muslims; she has helped protect them from invaders; and she has stopped the enemy in its tracks.

Mary's work as a protector of Christians has led more than a few priests to say that she wears combat boots. In the Litany of Our Lady of Sorrows, her titles include *Shield of the Oppressed, Conqueror of the incredulous, Protectress of those who fight, Haven of the shipwrecked, Calmer of tempests, Retreat of those who groan, Terror of the treacherous,* and *Standard-bearer of the Martyrs.* These are not titles of someone who is just sweet but not very helpful. She is more like a fierce momma-bear when she sees her cubs in trouble.

One of many examples of her helping her children in need happened in the little town of Pontmain, France, in 1871. At about 9 p.m., four children saw an apparition of Mary in the night sky. *They* could see her, but the adults could not. The people of Pontmain knew that an invading army, the Prussians, was going to attack the next day, and they were very scared but still tried to take care of things at home. When the children walked out of their barn, they could see Our Lady high in the sky smiling at them and wearing a dress covered in stars. During the apparition, Mary held up a banner that said the children's prayers had been heard by Jesus and were being answered. The next day, the invasion never came. The Prussians packed up, went home, and left France alone after that. What happened? The invading general wrote to his superiors that an "invisible Madonna" was blocking the road as they marched toward Pontmain. That was enough for the army to forget their battle in Pontmain and end the whole war with France.

There have been many other situations like this where Christians have prayed to Mary and received some kind of assistance, especially when they were outnumbered by the enemy. Mysteriously, their prayers are answered by a fog that rolls in or out, a change of wind, or some other surprising event that leads them to victory. Jesus and Mary always hear our prayers. We must not be afraid to ask, especially when we are scared.

Discussion Questions

Have you ever thought of Mary as a warrior before?

What do you think of the idea of Mary wearing combat boots like soldiers do? What color do you imagine they would be?

Why do you think Mary fights for her children?

Did You Know?

Many saints have spoken of how powerful the Rosary is. Blessed Pope Pius IX said, "Give me an army saying the Rosary and I will conquer the world." Other popes and holy people have declared that the Rosary is a weapon, such as Saint Pio (Padre Pio) and Blessed Jose Maria Escriva, the founder of Opus Dei. And Our Lady told Sister Lucia, one of the visionaries of the Fatima apparitions, that there is no material problem, but especially spiritual problem, that the Rosary could not solve in our age.

Prayers for the Day

Earliest Known Prayer to Mary

Beneath your compassion, we take refuge, O Mother of God:
do not despise our petitions in time of trouble:
but rescue us from dangers. Amen.

Hail Mary

Hail Mary, full of grace,
the Lord is with thee.
Blessed are thou among women,
and blessed is the fruit of thy womb, Jesus.

Holy Mary, Mother of God,
pray for us sinners now,
and at the hour of our death.
Amen.

Mary Is the Queen of Peace

There is something special about snow. Often, it arrives silently and without ceremony. One scarcely knows it is there. Only over time can you begin to see it, but the accumulation brings with it a blanket of beauty. Everything becomes different, suddenly pure, calm, quiet, and glistening with wonder. In a way, snow brings about a sense of peace.

This is much like the way Our Lady does things. Perhaps this is why Our Lady of the Snow is one of the oldest devotions to Mary, dating back to the year 350. On an August day, when it is usually about ninety-five degrees in Rome, snow fell on the ground mapping out where and how the Basilica of St. Mary Major should be built. The church was built exactly where the snow fell, measured by those who drew the boundaries before the snow had a chance to melt.

Our Lady is also often called the Queen of Peace. Like snow, she brings peace with her wherever she is called. Unlike snow, however, Mary doesn't want to merely cover over problems. She wants to get to the root of a problem, which usually goes back to the fact that people do not know and love God well enough. She always brings us back to him. And when we know God, there is peace in our hearts and justice in our communities.

During the apparition when Mary appeared to Juan Diego as Our Lady of Guadalupe, there was a great division among the native people of Mexico and the Spanish newcomers. The Spanish had forcibly taken over the area as Christian missionaries when they saw that the native Mexican people were doing many things that offended God a great deal. After these terrible things were stopped by the Spaniards, they tried, particularly the Franciscan missionary priests, to convert the native people to Catholicism. But the natives were very unhappy and did not like Catholicism because it represented the Spanish, whom they believed had taken too much from them (and many times they had—unfortunately, the Spanish did not always act in a Christian fashion). This tension brought on a great deal of conflict and even, at times, much violence.

So when Mary appeared to Juan Diego and left the beautiful image of herself on his *tilma,* or cloak, she was helping to heal the rift between the native people and the Spaniards. Through her image, the Spaniards saw her love and inspiration and grew deeper in their faith, mercy, and love. Meanwhile, the native people saw clearly in the image that she was the Mother of God—not a goddess to be worshipped, but an important mother to offer her help. Using images that the natives understood, like a belt around her belly, which signified that she was pregnant, they could "read" the image and see just who she was. It is estimated that between four and ten million conversions occurred because of that apparition in Mexico. There is no way to count how much the hearts of the Spaniards and the natives were touched by the apparition of Our Lady of Guadalupe, but we know it did a lot of miraculous things, including bringing peace to a very difficult region.

Discussion Questions

1. Why does Mary have the title Queen of Peace?

2. What is there about snow that can make us think of Mary?

3. In what ways do you think Mary as the Queen of Peace can help you, your family, and the world?

Did You Know?

The Rosary has a long history with its source in the 150 Psalms that were prayed every day by priests and religious. At a time in history when many could not read, the religious were encouraged to simply say 150 Our Fathers. To make their work easier, monks strung together beads so they could keep track of their Our Fathers. Through the prayers of St. Dominic, the Our Fathers were reduced to the beginning of each decade, or group of ten, and the 150 prayers became Hail Marys.

Prayers for the Day

Earliest Known Prayer to Mary

Beneath your compassion,
we take refuge, O Mother of God:
do not despise our petitions in time of trouble:
but rescue us from dangers.
Amen.

Hail Mary

Hail Mary, full of grace,
the Lord is with thee.
Blessed are thou among women,
and blessed is the fruit of thy womb, Jesus.

Holy Mary, Mother of God,
pray for us sinners now,
and at the hour of our death.
Amen.

Mary Helps With Everything

When Catherine Labouré was a little girl, her mother died. After the funeral, she went to her parent's room and took down a statue of Our Lady. She picked it up and said, "Now my mother is with you. You must become my mother." And that is exactly what happened.

When Catherine got older, she became a nun in Paris. One night, after everyone else in the convent was asleep, she was guided by an angel downstairs to the chapel. Praying as she waited, Catherine could hear the rustling of silk. When she looked up, she saw Mary dressed in a dazzling white silk dress.

There have been many apparitions of Mary throughout the centuries, but perhaps in no other one than this does she show herself to be most like a mother. She and Catherine spoke together for some time, as mothers and daughters do. During their discussion, Mary told Catherine that she would like to have a medal made to honor her and to help the world understand who she is and how much she wants to help us. This medal would become known as the Miraculous Medal, so named because of the all the miracles that have been associated with it. Catherine saw Mary several times and spoke of her beauty and her love. The French nun went on to be canonized a saint, not just because she saw Mary, but because she lived out the holy life that Mary helped guide her through as her spiritual mother.

Often times in our life, we struggle with something where we may not be quite sure what we need. Perhaps we need to go to sleep. Maybe we are hungry. Or maybe we are feeling sad or frustrated about something but don't know how to put it into words. Other times, we might feel that if we could just change one thing in our life, then everything would be perfect. We can feel empty and frustrated by the burdens we carry.

The best thing about Our Lady—and what is actually built right into this consecration as we entrust ourselves to her—is that she knows exactly what we need and when we need it. She knows when we need love and care or when we need to make sacrifices for others. Sometimes these things even happen at the same time since she loves us through the sacrifices we make. While we cannot always see her like St. Catherine Labouré did, we can be confident that she is working in very quiet but beautiful ways in our lives.

Later in this book, we will look at some of the clues we all have about what sort of mission God has in mind for us. But for now, try to consider the role Our Lady plays in your life to both help you become holy and become the person that God created you to be. Mary knows God's will for our lives and the mission he has for us. She will never lead us astray.

Discussion Questions

1. Why do you think Mary wants to help with everything we struggle with?

2. How do you think Mary can help you become who God wants you to be?

3. How can Mary help those who have lost their way and lost sight of what God has in mind for them?

Did You Know?

St. Theresa of Kolkata (Mother Teresa) used to pray ten *Memorare* prayers when she had an urgent need—nine for her request, and one more in thanksgiving because she knew her prayer would be heard and answered. Some call this the "emergency novena" for requests that need an immediate answer. This is the prayer she prayed:

> Remember, O most gracious Virgin Mary, that never was
> it known that anyone who fled to thy protection, implored
> thy help, or sought thine intercession was left unaided.

Inspired by this confidence, I fly unto thee, O Virgin of virgins, my mother; to thee do I come, before thee I stand, sinful and sorrowful. O Mother of the Word Incarnate, despise not my petitions, but in thy mercy hear and answer me. Amen.

Prayers for the Day

Earliest Known Prayer to Mary

Beneath your compassion,
we take refuge, O Mother of God:
do not despise our petitions in time of trouble:
but rescue us from dangers.
Amen.

Hail Mary

Hail Mary, full of grace,
the Lord is with thee.
Blessed are thou among women,
and blessed is the fruit of thy womb, Jesus.

Holy Mary, Mother of God,
pray for us sinners now,
and at the hour of our death.
Amen.

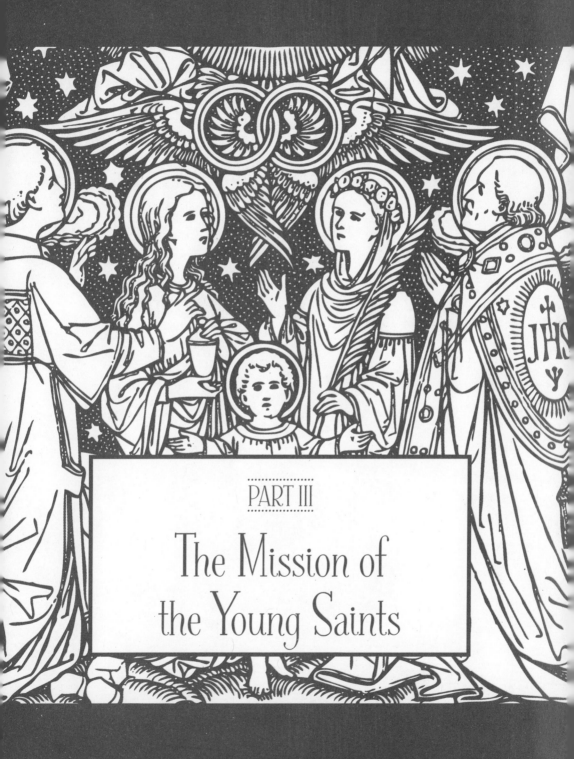

PART III

The Mission of the Young Saints

The Important Mission of Children

Young people often feel like they have very little to contribute to God or the world because of their age. "I'll do great things when I get older," they think. But there are great examples of very young people doing remarkable things for God.

C. S. Lewis made this clear in *The Chronicles of Narnia* through Lucy Pevensie. In *The Lion, The Witch, and The Wardrobe,* as well as in *Prince Caspian,* she is the youngest of the four children, and yet she is the one who sees Aslan first, is present when he is killed by the White Witch, and has the most confidence and trust in his assistance, even when others doubt.

Several times in the Bible, we hear how much Jesus loved children and how important children are in God's kingdom. He says things like "unless you turn and become like children, you will not enter the kingdom of heaven" (Mt 18:3), and in Mark, "whoever does not accept the kingdom of God like a child, will not enter it" (Mk 10:15).

For adults, our goal is to become like

children, to become childlike. There is a difference between childlike and childish. It is childish to throw a tantrum, it is childlike to trust wholly in God's plan for our lives. It is childish to only think of ourselves, it is childlike to notice the needs of others and want to attend to them, no matter the cost. Every Christian is striving for this childlike spirit, but a childlike spirit has a funny twist. It is only when we become childlike that we can actually become mature Christians, or most fully like Christ in our ability to trust, act charitably, and see with pure eyes. This is part of the reason why children have a great capacity to become holy and develop a deep relationship with God, because children are already childlike! St. Dominic Savio captured the idea well when he said, "I am not capable of doing big things, but I want to do everything, even the smallest things, for the greater glory of God."

For the next week, we will look at some examples of very mature Christians who had a tremendous impact on the world, even though they were just children.

Discussion Questions

1. Why do you think Jesus loved children so much?

2. Can you think of examples of people being childish?

3. What about examples of people being childlike? Take note of the difference between what you said here and what you said in #2.

Did You Know?

According to an ancient record written by Pope St. Leo III, it was a child who helped find the tomb of St. Anne. For many centuries, the tomb of the mother of Mary was lost after St. Anne's body had been moved by Christians escaping persecution in the Holy Lands. That changed on Easter in the year 792. Emperor Charlemagne was attending the consecration of a new church recently built over an older chapel in the town of Apt, France. During the Mass, a 14-year-old boy, born deaf, blind, and mute, made an uproar by walking up on the altar steps and repeatedly tapping his cane on a particular step. Because of his firm insistence and because it was out of character for the usually docile boy, a few men removed the step. Under it was a passageway that led to a subterranean corridor, or hallway. The emperor, the priests, the workmen, and the boy passed through it with torches until they reached another wall. The boy tapped there again and the workmen broke through it. They discovered yet another dark passage with a crypt at the end of it, where miraculously an oil lamp was burning. As the boy and the men drew near, the lamp went out, and the boy was instantly healed of his ailments. He cried out, "It is she!" When the crypt and casket were opened, a scroll was discovered inside announcing that it was the body of St. Anne.

Prayers for the Day

Prayer Taught to the Children at Fatima

Repeat 3 Times

My God, I believe, I adore, I hope, I love thee.
I ask pardon for those who do not believe, nor adore, nor hope, nor love thee.

Prayer of St. Aloysius Gonzaga to Our Lady

O holy Mary, my Mistress, into thy blessed trust and special keeping, into the bosom of thy tender mercy, this day, every day of my life and at the hour of my death, I commend my soul and body; to thee I entrust all my hopes and consolations, all my trials and miseries, my life and the end of my life, that through thy most holy intercession and thy merits, all my actions may be ordered and disposed according to thy will and that of thy divine Son. Amen.

Hail Mary

Hail Mary, full of grace,
the Lord is with thee.
Blessed are thou among women,
and blessed is the fruit of thy womb, Jesus.

Holy Mary, Mother of God,
pray for us sinners now,
and at the hour of our death.
Amen.

St. Bernadette Soubirous

You might think that the most powerful woman in the world would find powerful people to convey her message. Remarkably, this is exactly the opposite of what Our Lady does when she needs to deliver a message to the world.

On February 11, 1858, Mary made an important visit to the small town of Lourdes in a mountainous region of Southern France. She appeared to the fourteen-year-old peasant girl named Bernadette Soubirous who was gathering wood for her family's hearth near the old fortress of Massabielle. She was hardly what you might expect for a representative of Mary. In addition to being poorly educated and coming from a family that lived in deep poverty, Bernadette suffered regularly from various ailments, including asthma. Many years later, Bernadette said, "The Holy Virgin only chose me because I was the most ignorant. If she could have found someone else more ignorant, she would have chosen her."

Mary visited Bernadette eighteen times at the grotto in Lourdes. Four years prior, Pope Pius IX had declared that Mary was immaculately conceived—created without any sin on her soul. Part of Mary's message to Bernadette and the world was to confirm that she was the Immaculate Conception. Mary said "I am the Immaculate Conception" to Bernadette in her own dialect. Bernadette repeated these words to herself over and over, careful not to forget them, until she made her way to the bishop's house to relay Our Lady's message. The bishop then knew she was telling the truth about seeing Our Lady since there was no way for a girl like her to know what this title meant.

What was it about this sickly, poor, and ignorant peasant girl that Mary was attracted to? No doubt it was her humility and all the other things that were not perfect or powerful about her. Mary knew that her message would not be corrupted but believed. How could this ignorant girl make up such a tale, particularly with important names that she could hardly understand? As Christ revealed, "My grace is sufficient for you, for power is made perfect in weakness" (2 Cor 12:9).

During the apparitions, Our Lady asked Bernadette to dig in the dirt. As she dug, a spring bubbled up. This spring is the source of healing waters that still gush today, which countless pilgrims have bathed in to seek healing and peace.

In 1866, eight years after the first apparition, Bernadette moved away from Lourdes and became a nun in Nevers, France, where she would live the rest of her life. When she arrived, the other sisters were invited to ask her questions for one day about her miraculous apparitions, but never again after that. Bernadette told the sisters that she had merely been an instrument, much like a broom. She was able to help as God needed and then she was put away.

Bernadette died of tuberculosis at the age of thirty-five. Today, her body is incorrupt (meaning it has not suffered from decay) and can be viewed at the Chapel of Saint Gildard at the Sisters of Charity in Nevers.

Discussion Questions

1. Why do you think Mary chose Bernadette as her special messenger to the world?

2. Imagine Mary came to someone who is very proud. What might happen to her message?

3. Why do you think God would allow St. Bernadette's body to not decay after her death?

Did You Know?

Around a thousand years before St. Bernadette had her vision of Mary at Massabielle in Lourdes, a Muslim warrior named Mirat found his army surrounded by Christian soldiers who were trying to drive the Muslims out of Southern France. Mirat had made an oath that he would not surrender to a mortal man. After many weeks, the Christians were growing tired of waiting and the Muslims were slowly starving because they had no access to food. By chance, a bird dropped a fish into the fortress. Mirat, to try to trick the Christians into believing they still had plenty of food, threw the fish out of his stronghold. The local bishop, seeing Mirat's trick, thought of something new. He went to Mirat and said, "I know you have made an oath to never surrender to a mortal man, but would you surrender to the Queen of Heaven?" Mirat did surrender and he and all of his men became Christians. He took the name Lorus, which was changed a little and became the name for the famous village we now know as Lourdes.

Prayers for the Day

Prayer Taught to the Children at Fatima

Repeat 3 Times
My God, I believe, I adore, I hope, I love thee.
I ask pardon for those who do not believe, nor adore, nor hope, nor love thee.

Prayer of St. Aloysius Gonzaga to Our Lady

O holy Mary, my Mistress, into thy blessed trust and special keeping, into the bosom of thy tender mercy, this day, every day of my life and at the hour of my death, I commend my soul and body; to thee I entrust all my hopes and consolations, all my trials and miseries, my life and the end of my life, that through thy most holy intercession and thy merits, all my actions may be ordered and disposed according to thy will and that of thy divine Son. Amen.

Hail Mary

Hail Mary, full of grace,
the Lord is with thee.
Blessed are thou among women,
and blessed is the fruit of thy womb, Jesus.

Holy Mary, Mother of God,
pray for us sinners now,
and at the hour of our death.
Amen.

DAY 15

Sts. Jacinta and Francisco de Jesus Marto

These two saints, canonized in 2017, were brother and sister and two of the three children who witnessed the apparitions of Our Lady of Fatima. The third, Francisco and Jacinta's cousin Lucia, lived until 2005 and her cause for canonization is underway.

Francisco was born in 1908, with Jacinta following two years later. In 1916, as the children were out tending sheep, they experienced three apparitions of the Angel of Peace, who taught them the prayer included in the prayers for this week. The angel's visits served as a type of preparation for what would come next: Mary's visits.

The apparitions of Our Lady in Fatima started on May 13, 1917, with five more visits until the final apparition on October 13, 1917. During these apparitions, the Blessed Mother entrusted the children with many warnings for the world, predictions of things to come, and a course for the world to follow to avoid things worse than the First World War, which was going on at that time. Our Lady also showed them a vision of hell, as well as provided a remarkable miracle on her last visit in October when she made the sun twirl, change colors, and plunge from the sky. This miracle was witnessed by over seventy thousand people.

During her apparitions, Our Lady told Jacinta and Francisco that they would die young. Lucia had a different mission and would remain on earth much longer. The children were not afraid of death, however, because they knew Mary and had experienced her beauty, her love, and her comfort.

The children themselves went through many trials and showed a spiritual maturity well beyond their years. They diligently prayed the Rosary, attended Mass, and adored the Eucharist in the way taught to them by the Angel of Peace, flat on the floor with their heads down.

Shortly before Francisco's death, Our Lady appeared to the siblings and told them that they would die soon. We have a record of what Jacinta told Lucia after the visit:

> Look, Lucia, Our Lady came to see us and said that she was coming soon for Francisco. She asked me if I still wanted to convert more sinners. I said yes. Our Lady wants me to go to two hospitals but it is not to cure me. It is to suffer more for the love of God, the conversion of sinners and in reparation for the offenses committed against the Immaculate Heart of Mary. She told me that you would not go with me. My mother will take me there and afterwards I am to be left there alone.

Just as they were told, both children contracted the dreaded Spanish Flu. Francisco's illness did not last long and he died on April 4, 1919 at the age of ten.

Jacinta continued to suffer dreadful surgeries and complications from the deadly influenza for months. She said she suffered willingly for sinners of the world. As she had been told, Jacinta died alone in the hospital on February 20, 1920 at the age of nine.

The children willingly suffered all these things with the consolation that they were helping to save souls from hell. Since Mary had shown them hell, they were even more intent upon doing whatever it took to save souls from that terrible, terrible place.

Discussion Questions

1. The Angel of Peace came before Our Lady did. Why do you think he came first?

2. Why do you think the children were so willing to suffer for Mary's work?

3. How do you think you would feel if Our Lady appeared to you?

Did You Know?

The first part of the *Hail Mary* prayer comes from two parts in the Gospel of Luke: first, when the angel Gabriel addresses Mary to ask her if she is willing to be the mother of Jesus, and second, when St. Elizabeth greets Mary and the child in her womb (St. John the Baptist) leaps for joy at the approach of the Messiah in Mary's womb. But what about the second half of this most special prayer? "Holy Mary, Mother of God, pray for us sinners now and at the hour of our death" came about during the terrible fourteenth-century plague called the Black Death. Many people died very quickly from the fast-spreading plague, so those that lived wondered if they, too, might die soon. From their own uncertainty about how long they may live, the second half of the prayer that we now know as the Hail Mary was added, although it was not *officially* added by the Church until the Rosary prayers were codified in the sixteenth century.

Prayers for the Day

Prayer Taught to the Children at Fatima

Repeat 3 Times
My God, I believe, I adore, I hope, I love thee.
I ask pardon for those who do not believe, nor adore, nor hope, nor love thee.

Prayer of St. Aloysius Gonzaga to Our Lady

O holy Mary, my Mistress, into thy blessed trust and special keeping, into the bosom of thy tender mercy, this day, every day of my life and at the hour of my death, I commend my soul and body; to thee I entrust all my hopes and consolations, all my trials and miseries, my life and the end of my life, that through thy most holy intercession and thy merits, all my actions may be ordered and disposed according to thy will and that of thy divine Son. Amen.

Hail Mary

Hail Mary, full of grace,
the Lord is with thee.
Blessed are thou among women,
and blessed is the fruit of thy womb, Jesus.

Holy Mary, Mother of God,
pray for us sinners now,
and at the hour of our death.
Amen.

St. Aloysius Gonzaga

The oldest of seven children, Aloysius (or Luigi in Italian) Gonzaga was born in 1568 to a noble family in northern Italy. His father was a nobleman, called a marquis, and his mother was both a baron's daughter as well as a lady in waiting to Queen Isabel, the wife of King Phillip II of Spain.

At the age of eight, Aloysius was sent to serve in the court of Francesco I de Medici, the Grand Duke of Tuscany, to further his education. But while there, he developed a kidney disease that forced him to often stay in bed. During his illness, he read about the saints and spent much time in prayer. He was also discouraged by the course language and lives of the nobles around him, so at age nine he took a vow of chastity, or purity.

Aloysius then met the future saint and Jesuit priest Charles Borromeo, who gave him his first Communion. The influence of St. Charles and a book he read about Jesuits in India led Aloysius to the idea of becoming a Jesuit.

It wasn't until the family moved to Spain that Aloysius acted upon his desire to become a priest. His mother was okay with his decision, but his father was furious and tried to prevent him from what he saw as throwing his life away. Other family members tried to persuade him to at least become a diocesan priest because then he could still keep his fortune and become a bishop. But Aloysius had no interest in becoming powerful. He wanted to be a missionary.

After joining the Jesuits and renouncing his inheritance, he suffered greatly from his kidney problems, a skin disease, frequent headaches, and sleeping troubles. Aloysius took his final vows as a Jesuit in 1587 at the age of nineteen. For the next several years, he studied under the spiritual direction of another Jesuit saint and priest, Robert Bellarmine. In 1590, after just a few years of being a priest, Aloysius had a vision of the archangel Gabriel who told him that he would die within a year.

In 1591, a plague broke out and Aloysius helped bathe the sick and prepared them for death. He confessed to Fr. Bellarmine that it was very difficult work and that he had to work hard to overcome his repulsion of the smells and sights of those dying from the terrible disease.

Soon after, Aloysius contracted the awful plague and died during the octave of Corpus Christi, confirming the vision given to him by the archangel. His demeanor was so pleasant in death, few believed that he was close to dying. He was beatified in 1605 and canonized a saint in 1726 along with another young saint we will meet soon, Stanislaw Kostka.

Aloysius was born into a very noble family, whose name was known far and wide. Ironically, while his father was disappointed that his son did not become a powerful nobleman or bishop, Aloysius's name is the one everyone remembers today. Many Churches, chapels, and schools bear his name around the world, including Gonzaga University in Washington State, best known for their basketball team.

Most of the images of St. Aloysius include a Rosary because his devotion to the Virgin Mary was so strong. We can see more evidence of how devoted he was to her in the prayer he wrote that we are reading this week.

Discussion Questions

1. Why didn't Aloysius's father want him to become a priest?

2. What role do you think Aloysius's illness made in his discovery of his vocation?

3. Why did Aloysius's legacy outlive that of his family?

Did You Know?

When we hear the name Mercedes, most of us think of the car; few know the connection it has to Mary. The Mercedes car brand came about when a wealthy Austrian diplomat, Emil Jellineck, financed a new company to make racing cars. He named it after his daughter, Mercedes Jellineck. But the name Mercedes comes from a Spanish name for Mary, Our Lady of Ransom or Our Lady of Mercies *(La Virgen de la Merced or Nuestra Señora de las Mercede)*. The name came about when the Muslim invaders enslaved many Christians in Spain. A religious order of men dedicated to Our Lady was formed to help free the captive Christians from slavery, calling themselves the Mercederians, or the Order of the Blessed Virgin Mary of Mercy.

It is this long history and connection to Our Lady's powerful intercession that gave the car company its beautiful name.

Prayers for the Day

Prayer Taught to the Children at Fatima

Repeat 3 Times
My God, I believe, I adore, I hope, I love thee.
I ask pardon for those who do not believe, nor adore, nor hope, nor love thee.

Prayer of St. Aloysius Gonzaga to Our Lady

O holy Mary, my Mistress, into thy blessed trust and special keeping, into the bosom of thy tender mercy, this day, every day of my life and at the hour of my death, I commend my soul and body; to thee I entrust all my hopes and consolations, all my trials and miseries, my life and the end of my life, that through thy most holy intercession and thy merits, all my actions may be ordered and disposed according to thy will and that of thy divine Son. Amen.

Hail Mary

Hail Mary, full of grace,
the Lord is with thee.
Blessed are thou among women,
and blessed is the fruit of thy womb, Jesus.

Holy Mary, Mother of God,
pray for us sinners now,
and at the hour of our death.
Amen.

DAY 17

Little Nellie Organ

If you're like most children today, you received or will receive your first Communion around the age of seven. This was not always the case. For many centuries, twelve was the earliest a child could receive Holy Communion. But there was a tiny little girl in Ireland who helped get the first Communion age changed for all of us.

Ellen Organ, nicknamed Nellie, was born in 1903. The youngest of four children, she showed signs of a great love for God from a very early age, insisting on calling him "Holy God" at the age of two. Tragedy struck the family when Nellie's mother died of tuberculosis. Nellie's father, a soldier in the Irish military, quickly realized that he could not properly care for all the children, so they were divided up and sent to live with religious communities. Nellie and her sister were taken in by the Good Shepherd Sisters. The little girl said to the kind sisters who cared for her, "Holy God took my mudder, but he has given me you to be my mudder." In addition to losing her mother, Nellie also suffered a lot of physical pain, including a back that was out of joint. It was soon discovered that she had the dreaded disease that killed her mother and that she had only a short time to live.

What was extraordinary about Nellie, however, was her very advanced understanding of theological concepts at such a young age, as well as her deep embrace of the suffering given to her, which was truly torturous at times. During her greatest sufferings, Nellie would lay her arms across her body and remind herself how much worse Christ's suffering must have been.

At the tender age of four, Nellie had a deep longing to be united with Holy God in the Eucharist. Even if she could not receive communion, she asked her nurse to come to her right after receiving and to kiss her so that she could be as close to Jesus as possible. This ardent desire was explained to a priest who then tested Nellie's knowledge about the Eucharist. Her answers showed a remarkable awareness of the spiritual reality. Although her answers were simple, they were profound. "Jesus goes down my throat and into my heart," she told the priest. She was eventually granted the grace of being able to receive Communion, which caused her to shed many tears of joy.

Nellie also loved Mary and was devoted to the Rosary, saying it slowly and with great attention. She also loved her statue of the Infant of Prague, going to adoration, and fresh flowers (not fake flowers which she thought were too stiff). "Isn't Holy God good to have made such lovely flowers for me?" she is known to have said.

Tuberculosis finally took Nellie's life on February 2, 1908. Pope Saint Pius X, after hearing about Nellie's devotion for the Eucharist, said, "There! That is the sign for which I was waiting." The saintly pope officially changed the age for receiving Communion in 1910, less than two years after Nellie's death.

Discussion Questions

1. Nellie's life involved so much tragedy. How did she deal with all these terrible things?

2. Little Nellie died before she was five. In what ways was her behavior different from most kids that age?

3. Are there things you can do to be more like Nellie when you suffer?

Did You Know?

At many churches, particularly in Europe and in Central and South America, you can find votive offerings to Our Lady. A votive offering is a way of saying "thank you" for prayers answered. Many of these offerings include proof of real healings, such as crutches, eyeglasses, and leg braces left behind by people that no longer need them. Others have left paintings or photographs depicting the miraculous healings. One church in Italy, called Our Lady of Ghisallo, is full of bicycles from the many cyclists who have been protected from harm through Mary's intercession.

Prayers for the Day

Prayer Taught to the Children at Fatima

Repeat 3 Times

My God, I believe, I adore, I hope, I love thee.
I ask pardon for those who do not believe, nor adore, nor hope, nor love thee.

Prayer of St. Aloysius Gonzaga to Our Lady

O holy Mary, my Mistress, into thy blessed trust and special keeping, into the bosom of thy tender mercy, this day, every day of my life and at the hour of my death, I commend my soul and body; to thee I entrust all my hopes and consolations, all my trials and miseries, my life and the end of my life, that through thy most holy intercession and thy merits, all my actions may be ordered and disposed according to thy will and that of thy divine Son. Amen.

Hail Mary

Hail Mary, full of grace,
the Lord is with thee.
Blessed are thou among women,
and blessed is the fruit of thy womb, Jesus.

Holy Mary, Mother of God,
pray for us sinners now,
and at the hour of our death.
Amen.

St. Therese of the Child Jesus

The fifth of five girls, Therese Martin was born in 1873. A very strong-willed child, Therese would scream if she did not get her way. Therese later admitted while living in a convent that she was far from being the perfect child.

Therese's mother died of cancer when she was just three. That experience changed her dramatically, and she became very sensitive and preferred to hide rather than be noticed by people. Her hiddenness continued when she went to school and was bullied by an older girl because she was smart for her young age. Therese took to hiding to deal with her sadness and avoid the bully. She dreamed of Jesus taking her away to some desert.

When she was nine, her older sister Pauline, who had been like a second mother to her, joined the convent of Carmel. Therese was devastated by her sister's move to the convent and felt as though her sister was lost to her, just as her mother had been many years before.

Around Christmas of 1886, Therese was unburdened from the sadness and stress she had carried with her since her mother died. "God worked a little miracle to make me grow up in an instant. . . . On that blessed night . . . Jesus, who saw fit to make Himself a child out of love for me, saw fit to have me come forth from the swaddling clothes and imperfections of childhood."

Therese's new maturity showed itself in dramatic ways. She too felt called to join Pauline at Carmel, where her other sister, Marie, had also gone. Still too young to join the convent, Therese prayed and looked for a way to be able to join Carmel even at her tender age. Upon visiting the pope in Rome, Leo XIII told her, "Well, my child, do what the superiors decide. . . . You will enter if it is God's will." Apparently, it *was* God's will, as the bishop of Bayeux gave Therese permission to enter Carmel at the age of fifteen.

Finally, Therese found the desert that Jesus had taken her to so she could hide with him in Carmel. And like the desert, it was a dry and difficult life. She suffered through many misunderstandings and grudges from other nuns, but eventually made her final vows as a Carmelite.

During her time at Carmel, Therese developed what would come to be called "the little way." Due to her vows of obedience, she could not do great things, but she could do small things with great love. She explained, "Love proves itself by deeds, so how am I to show my love? Great deeds are forbidden me. The only way I can prove my love is by scattering flowers and these flowers are every little sacrifice, every glance and word, and the doing of the least actions for love."

Therese understood that staying small and childlike was the best way to allow Jesus to get her to heaven. "Your arms, My Jesus, are the elevator which will take me to Heaven," she once said. "There is no need for me to grow up; on the contrary, I must stay little, and become more and more so."

Like St. Bernadette and Little Nellie, Therese also came down with tuberculosis. She died on September 30, 1897. After the discovery of her spiritual writing *The Story of a Soul*, and after many miracles were connected to her, the cause for her sainthood started. She was beatified in 1923 and, just two years later, was canonized a saint. In 1997 Pope John Paul II declared her a Doctor of the Church.

Throughout her life, St. Therese had a deep devotion to Our Lady and referred to herself as "the Little Flower of the Blessed Virgin." When she was ten, Therese consecrated herself to Mary. Later, she wrote of the experience saying, "Doubtless I was chosen for this (consecration) because I was left without my mother on earth. . . . In consecrating myself to the Virgin Mary, I asked her to watch over me, placing into the act all the devotion of my soul, and it seemed to me, I saw her once again looking down and smiling on her 'little flower.'"

Discussion Questions

1. In what ways do you think St. Therese is different than other saints?

2. What was it about being small that she liked?

3. Why do you think Therese is called The Little Flower?

Did You Know?

Prior to her death, Therese declared that she would spend her heaven doing good on earth. Frequently, prayers directed to her, especially novenas, will receive a rose (or roses) as confirmation that the prayer has been heard. Sometimes she even delivers roses that are drawn or made of paper.

Prayers for the Day

Prayer Taught to the Children at Fatima

Repeat 3 Times
My God, I believe, I adore, I hope, I love thee.
I ask pardon for those who do not believe, nor adore, nor hope, nor love thee.

Prayer of St. Aloysius Gonzaga to Our Lady

O holy Mary, my Mistress, into thy blessed trust and special keeping, into the bosom of thy tender mercy, this day, every day of my life and at the hour of my death, I commend my soul and body; to thee I entrust all my hopes and consolations, all my trials and miseries, my life and the end of my life, that through thy most holy intercession and thy merits, all my actions may be ordered and disposed according to thy will and that of thy divine Son. Amen.

Hail Mary

Hail Mary, full of grace,
the Lord is with thee.
Blessed are thou among women,
and blessed is the fruit of thy womb, Jesus.

Holy Mary, Mother of God,
pray for us sinners now,
and at the hour of our death.
Amen.

St. Stanislaus Kostka

Stanislaus Kostka's life is very similar to a saint we've already met, St. Aloysius of Gonzaga. Although born in Poland, the second of seven children, his family moved to Vienna where Stanislaus and his brother attended Jesuit schools. Stanislaus excelled in his studies, was loved for his cheerfulness, and most of all, grew deeper in his devotion to Jesus.

During his beatification, his older brother Paul, who was able to attend, reported that Stanislaus "devoted himself so completely to spiritual things that he frequently became unconscious, especially in the church of the Jesuit Fathers at Vienna. It is true, that this had happened at home to my brother at Easter when he was seated at table with our parents and other persons."

Although Stanislaus's brother had nice things to say during his beatification, things were not always so rosy between them. When they were young, Paul frequently yelled and beat up Stanislaus. It became so bad that Stanislaus warned Paul his abusive habits would one day drive Stanislaus far from home. But like so many things, God was able to turn the terrible abuse he experienced into something good.

Stanislaus felt drawn to the Jesuit order and hoped to join their ranks, but his father did not look kindly upon the new order. If Stanislaus felt called to holy orders, his father preferred something more established and esteemed. Stanislaus determined, with the help of his spiritual director, that he would have to join the Jesuit Order in Rome because the province in Vienna required his father's permission until he reached a certain age. This, combined with the beatings his brother was giving him, prompted him to leave home and set out on the long, 1,500-mile journey to Rome, and he did so on foot!

Many months later, exhausted and sickly, Stanislaus finally arrived in Rome. On October 29, 1567, his seventeenth birthday, he was finally able to join the Jesuit Order. In less than a year, his health deteriorated so much that he was near death. On August 10, Stanislaus's illness worsened and he knew his life on earth was coming to an end. That day, he wrote a letter to Our Lady asking for the gift of being able to celebrate the feast of the Assumption with her in heaven. And at about 4 a.m. on August 15, 1568, the feast of the Assumption, he went home to his reward. He was eighteen.

All of Rome, hearing about this very pious young Jesuit, recognized his sanctity and venerated his remains. He was immediately considered a saint in Italy and Poland, and many miracles were associated with the site of his tomb.

As for his older brother, Paul spent years living with great remorse for the way he had treated Stanislaus. He was jubilant as he attended his little brother's beatification and intended to join the Jesuits himself but died suddenly on the day he was to enter. St. Stanislaus's body was discovered to be incorrupt many years after his death.

Discussion Questions

1. What role did Paul play in Stanislaus's vocation to the Jesuits?

2. How do you think Paul felt when he attended the beatification of his younger brother?

3. Like many saints, Stanislaus's life was a mix between suffering and the miraculous. Why do you think this happens so often among the lives of the saints?

Did You Know?

Many churches are named for Mary around the world. In Rome alone, there are ninety! Their names often reflect something important that she did for the city, like Santa Maria del Popolo (St. Mary of the People), built around the year 1000 to assure the local population that the ghost of the bad emperor Nero was not haunting them. Other churches represent a beautiful quality about her, such has Our Lady of Good Counsel, while still others emphasize the way she conquers false gods, like Santa Maria Sopra Minerva (St. Mary's over Minerva). Minerva was a Roman goddess whose temple was on that site a millennia ago, overcome by the goodness and sanctity of the Mother of God.

Prayers for the Day

Prayer Taught to the Children at Fatima

Repeat 3 Times

My God, I believe, I adore, I hope, I love thee.
I ask pardon for those who do not believe, nor adore, nor hope, nor love thee.

Prayer of St. Aloysius Gonzaga to Our Lady

O holy Mary, my Mistress, into thy blessed trust and special keeping, into the bosom of thy tender mercy, this day, every day of my life and at the hour of my death, I commend my soul and body; to thee I entrust all my hopes and consolations, all my trials and miseries, my life and the end of my life, that through thy most holy intercession and thy merits, all my actions may be ordered and disposed according to thy will and that of thy divine Son. Amen.

Hail Mary

Hail Mary, full of grace,
the Lord is with thee.
Blessed are thou among women,
and blessed is the fruit of thy womb, Jesus.

Holy Mary, Mother of God,
pray for us sinners now,
and at the hour of our death.
Amen.

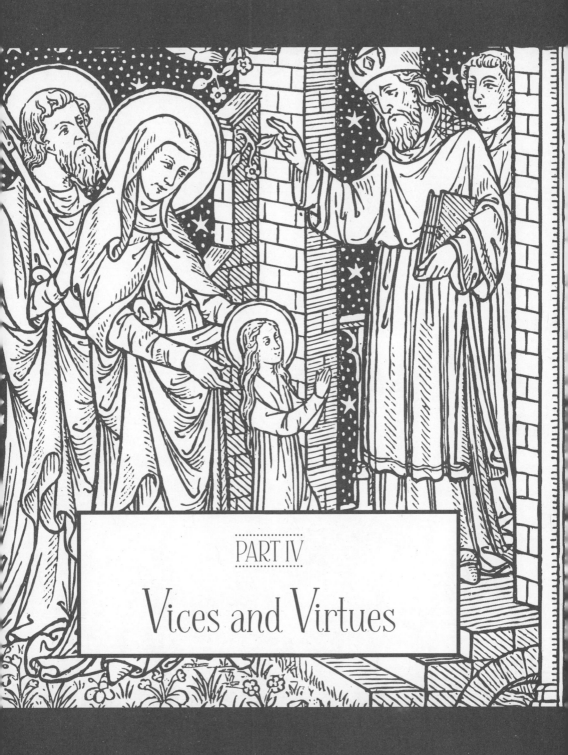

PART IV

Vices and Virtues

What Are Virtues and Vices?

In his famous work about Mary, *True Devotion to Mary*, St. Louis de Montfort says that Mary will help our virtues grow. But what exactly are virtues?

Each one of us is born with different gifts. Some of our gifts are called virtues. Virtue comes from the Latin word *virtus*, which describes a habit that prompts us toward morally good actions. For example, being patient or courageous is a virtue and the person who has these virtues has the ability to act well, even when it is difficult. Virtues are like our spiritual muscles. If we don't use them, then we don't become strong. God knows this, so in life we often have to struggle against difficult situations to help our virtues grow. We can't become courageous if we don't have problems in our life that require us to act courageously. Perhaps you feel like the same kinds of struggles pop up in your life; for example, do you have a hard time sharing with your brothers and sisters or with your classmates? If so, you likely have a great gift, a virtue, of generosity in your soul, but you must learn to control your greed so that you can live generously. St. Ignatius of Loyola taught this, that the very things we struggle with are clues to the gifts God has planted in our souls. These virtues will be qualities we must increase in order to perform the work God has given us to do in this life.

What happens if we don't act in a virtuous way when difficult problems arise? Then we get stuck in what are called vices. Vices are the things that make our soul weak, much like a body that never exercises. We can't do the things we want if we don't have strong virtues, so we get stuck doing the things we don't want to do because of our vices. Most people will never be completely free of all vices, but we can work hard to develop our spiritual muscles so we can do the things we want to do.

The vices are usually grouped into what are called the seven deadly sins. These are the vices that categorize most sins, such as pride, greed, gluttony, and so on. We will look at many of these over the next week to understand how we can avoid them and grow our spiritual muscles, the virtues.

While we don't talk very much about the virtues today, they have a long history in the Catholic faith and even before. The ancient Greeks saw the virtues as the path to finding happiness. Catholics then took this idea and made it fit with Christian teaching. The virtues are the way to happiness because they help us become holy, and holiness is the path to true happiness with God in heaven. Even today, when the Church considers someone for sainthood, the person's life is looked at to see if they lived the virtues heroically. If so, they are one step closer to being named a saint.

This week we are going to look at specific kinds of vices that almost every human being has struggled against, as well as the opposite virtue that allows us to live freely and happily.

Discussion Questions

1. Can we acquire virtues without any kind of struggle or temptation?

2. How are virtues like muscles in our body?

3. How can our struggles help us to figure out what our greatest virtues might be?

Did You Know?

Perhaps your parents or grandparents remember the show *Gilligan's Island*. It was a show about seven people who went on a three-hour boat tour and somehow got shipwrecked on an island. The show was built around their efforts to be rescued, but because each of the characters represents a different vice, they are always foiled by someone's weakness. The Skipper, for example, suffered from anger and was always yelling at Gilligan; Thurston Howell was greedy, only worrying about his money; and MaryAnn was filled with envy because of the attention the movie star, Ginger, was always getting.

Prayers for the Day

Prayer Taught to the Children at Fatima

Repeat 3 Times

My God, I believe, I adore, I hope, I love thee.
I ask pardon for those who do not believe, nor adore, nor hope, nor love thee.

Hail Mary

Repeat 10 times

Hail Mary, full of grace,
the Lord is with thee.
Blessed are thou among women,
and blessed is the fruit of thy womb, Jesus.

Holy Mary, Mother of God,
pray for us sinners now,
and at the hour of our death.
Amen.

DAY 21

Disobedience and Obedience

When preparing for our first confession, there are many sins we can think about, but the best place to start is the first sin of Adam and Eve. You probably know the story of the first man and woman who were tempted by the serpent to eat the fruit of the tree God had told them not to eat. Their sin boiled down to being disobedient to God. They didn't exactly know *why* he told them not to eat from it, other than that their eyes would be opened, but they had to trust him. Adam and Eve knew that God knew what was best for them.

Some of our sins happen because we do the wrong thing at the wrong time or in the wrong way, but many of our sins also boil down to disobedience to someone who has authority over us. Do you always listen to what your mother and father tell you to do? Do you obey your teachers? Do you ignore the penance the priest gives you after confession? Someone with an obedient heart avoids life's struggles. Why? Because they trust when they are obedient to the Church, or to their parents who represent God in the life of the child, they know they are on the safest path. Imagine how much easier things could be if Adam and Eve, and every human after them, had been obedient to God.

One of my favorite books when I was a child was *A Fish Out of Water.* In this story, a

97

young boy gets a fish at a pet store, and the store owner, Mr. Carp, warns him to feed the fish only a pinch, never more, "or something may happen. You never know what." The young boy, however, thinks that giving his new fish, Otto, just a pinch isn't enough, so he pours a whole bunch more fish food into the bowl. Sure enough, the fish starts to grow. In fact, he grows so big the boy has to put him in a huge vase; then a giant pot; then the bathtub; then finally the fish is washed into the basement when the tub overflows.

Desperate for help, the boy calls for help and the fire department comes. Otto is taken to the local pool, but even there he just keeps growing. Finally, Mr. Carp shows up with a bag of tools and a snorkel and dives into the pool. A moment later, Otto suddenly disappears, and Mr. Carp emerges from the pool with the fish back to his regular size, now swimming in a fish bowl. No one really knows how he did it, but everyone is grateful that there is no longer a giant fish in the swimming pool. Mr. Carp returns the fish bowl to the boy, along with a stern warning not to overfeed the tiny creature again.

Like the boy found out with his fish, obedience wasn't just about listening to Mr. Carp because he was a grown up, but listening to him because it was best for the boy and for his fish. If he had listened, the whole mess wouldn't have happened.

Our lives can be a lot like the young boy. Jesus knew that we wouldn't be very good at doing what we're supposed to do, which is why he gave us confession to help correct our mistakes. He gave priests the ability to forgive and absolve our sins, even if we don't know exactly how this happens on a technical level. This is similar to Mr. Carp's rescue of Otto. We don't know exactly how he shrunk Otto, but he did. And then the priest often gives us guidance about how to avoid future sin, much like Mr. Carp told the boy how to keep Otto small. Although it has some mystery to it, confession is a very practical way to clean up the messes in our lives.

We won't always understand why we are not allowed to do certain things, but we must learn—no matter what our age—that we just have to trust people like Mr. Carp, like our priests and our parents, because they know why we shouldn't do something. They want to help us avoid certain things so we don't have to find out the hard way. Just like God loves obedient children, so, too, do mothers and fathers; and so does our spiritual mother, Mary.

Mary's life also offers us a model of perfect obedience. While Eve said "no" to God's request, Mary corrected Eve's disobedience with her "yes." It was this yes, this obedient act, that allowed Christ to come to us. Mary's obedience brought a great good to the world. Our obedience can also bring great blessings to the world.

Discussion Questions

1. What was Adam and Eve's first sin?

2. Why is obedience important?

3. What should you try to remember about obedience when it is hard to do?

Did You Know?

St. Albert the Great (1200–1280) was a brilliant philosopher and a theologian in the thirteenth century who was said to have been given his strong mind and keen insights by Our Lady. Later in his life, as Albert was getting older, Mary took the gift of his fine mind away to make it clear that it truly was a gift. But when his dear friend St. Thomas Aquinas needed to be defended, she gave it back to him for a short time so he could stand up for his friend.

Prayers for the Day

Prayer Taught to the Children at Fatima

Repeat 3 Times
My God, I believe, I adore, I hope, I love thee.
I ask pardon for those who do not believe, nor adore, nor hope, nor love thee.

Hail Mary

Repeat 10 times
Hail Mary, full of grace,
the Lord is with thee.
Blessed are thou among women,
and blessed is the fruit of thy womb, Jesus.

Holy Mary, Mother of God,
pray for us sinners now,
and at the hour of our death.
Amen.

Greed and Generosity

reed is the vice of being focused too much on things, whether it's money, or jewels, or even just one ring, like in *The Lord of the Rings* by J. R. R. Tolkien. Tolkien, a Catholic author, wrote *The Lord of the Rings* with the same basic moral laws of our world, so things like murder and stealing are both very bad for the souls of his characters, as is greed. In the character of Gollum, Tolkien shows what happens to our souls when we are fixed on having something other than God. In Gollum's case, it was the ring, which he referred to as "my precious."

Gollum once was a hobbit named Smeagol and encountered the ring when it was owned by someone else. Smeagol had to have that ring and ended up murdering his hobbit friend who owned it. It was greed that led him to murder his friend; likewise, it was greed that led to his unreasonable fear of losing the ring after he got it in his hands. Both of these deformed his character dramatically.

Things got even worse when Smeagol lost the ring. He was slowly transformed into a shadow of his former self and was renamed Gollum to reveal how dramatic the transformation was. He was unrecognizable as Smeagol and had become a naked, ugly, bald, scrawny, and deformed hobbit.

In the second book of *The Lord of the Rings*, *The Twin Towers*, the personalities of Gollum and Smeagol continue to live on in the same person. The vice of greed has made one person act like two people constantly warring with each other. Gollum has this dialogue with himself: "Where iss it, where iss it: my Precious, my Precious? It's ours, it is, and we wants it. The thieves, the thieves, the filthy little thieves. Where are they with the Precious? . . . We hates them." You can see that he's living with this "double-life" inside because he's calling himself "we." (Spoiler Alert) In the end, Gollum's desire for the ring was what killed him. He snagged it from Frodo and then fell into the fiery pit at Mordor. Finally, the One Ring—and the warring Smeagol and Gollum—is gone, once and for all.

Charlie and the Chocolate Factory offers another great glimpse into the vice of greed. With the exception of Charlie Bucket, all of the children who win golden tickets have many vices, but greed is most apparent in Veruca Salt. Veruca wants just about everything, and she wants it now! Just like Gollum, her part in the chocolate tour ends with a tantrum to get a golden egg. In a raging tantrum, she makes a mess of the room they are in and finally jumps up onto the scale that determines if an egg is good or bad. She was declared a bad egg and promptly fell down the garbage chute. While we are assured her fall didn't kill her, Veruca certainly did not get what she wanted, nor the lifetime supply of chocolate.

The opposite of greed is generosity. When we place God above everything else, we know that he is in charge of our lives. We know that he has given us many gifts and we are called to share them with others. Rather than being enslaved by material "stuff," we are freed through his gifts to be generous and mindful of the needs of others.

Mary, because of her perfect generosity, is then truly the freest of all humans because she was never enslaved by things and generously responded to God's requests. When the angel Gabriel asked her if she would consent to being the mother of Jesus, she generously said "yes" without counting what it might cost her.

Discussion Questions

1. Have you ever wanted something so much that you did bad things to get it?

2. Why do vices like greed destroy us if we want them more than we want God?

3. How do you think Mary could help you overcome greed?

Did You Know?

Two characters in J. R. R. Tolkien's work *The Lord of the Rings* are representations of the Virgin Mary: Eowyn and the elf queen Galadriel. Eowyn is a royal shield-maid with tremendous courage. Queen Galadriel is majestic and helpful to those in need, like when she appeared to Samwise Gamgee who was near despair in a black spider's lair. About beauty, Tolkien once explained, "All my own small perception of beauty both in majesty and simplicity is founded upon Our Lady."

Prayers for the Day

Prayer Taught to the Children at Fatima

Repeat 3 Times
My God, I believe, I adore, I hope, I love thee.
I ask pardon for those who do not believe, nor adore, nor hope, nor love thee.

Hail Mary

Repeat 10 times
Hail Mary, full of grace,
the Lord is with thee.
Blessed are thou among women,
and blessed is the fruit of thy womb, Jesus.

Holy Mary, Mother of God,
pray for us sinners now,
and at the hour of our death.
Amen.

Gluttony and Temperance

Gluttony is the vice of eating or drinking too much. One of my favorite characters who struggles much with gluttony is the dear Winnie the Pooh. One story tells us of poor Pooh spending a morning enjoying his fill of honey before making his way to Rabbit's house for tea, where he enjoys even more honey. After tea, Pooh gets stuck in the same hole he used to enter Rabbit's house earlier that day. Rabbit's hospitality has put his waistline over the edge, and Pooh discovers that he simply cannot budge out of that hole.

There was nothing to be done but let Pooh hang there in the hole until he lost a few inches off that tummy. So there he hung, his head outside facing the forest while his feet remained inside Rabbit's cozy home. He was there long enough for Rabbit to notice that his feet made a rather nice towel hook. But eventually, Pooh makes his way out of the rabbit hole, a thinner and wiser bear—or so we hope.

One of the realities that Pooh discovered quite literally is that gluttony gets us stuck. When we eat or drink too much, not only is it not good for our bodies, but it is even worse for our souls. Pooh, as a bear, doesn't have a soul, but we do. When we give into the temptations of good food and drink, our bodies gain more control over our decisions than our souls do. But it is our souls that should be in charge! Slowly, gluttony makes us slaves to our appetites so that we, like Pooh, get stuck doing what we don't really want to do.

We also see gluttony in *Charlie and the Chocolate Factory* in the person of Augustus Gloop, who is fixated on eating. About the most we hear out of the lucky golden ticket winner is that he his hungry. It is no surprise, then, that his tour of the famed chocolate factory ends when he leans into the great chocolate river and helps himself to the warm flowing liquid. Of course, if you are familiar with this story, you know that he falls in and gets sucked into the great network of chocolate tubes.

The opposite of gluttony is the virtue of temperance. Temperance means that we listen to our interior signs, such as a full stomach, which tell us we have had enough to eat. Temperance allows our mind and will to take control of what we eat and drink, rather than our bellies. When our soul is in charge, then we have real freedom.

The Virgin Mary, in her temperance, was never gluttonous; she never overate or drank too much. While not recorded in the Bible, it is easy to imagine that Mary fasted—skipping meals or certain foods—to offer further sacrifices to God for sinners. Food, when used well (both when eating or abstaining), is a tremendous blessing for our bodies, souls, and even the souls of others.

Discussion Questions

1. What could Pooh have done differently to not get himself stuck in Rabbit's hole?

2. What's wrong with having too much of something?

3. What does it mean to be temperate?

Did You Know?

Many plants, flowers, and herbs have been named for Mary. In England, Marigolds, or "Mary's gold," are known as Our Lady's Dowry. Roses have also long been a symbol for her, while lilies represent the Annunciation, when the angel Gabriel came to announce the incarnation of Christ. Rosemary, mint, lemon balm, and many other plants have connections to Mary, so much so that Mary gardens have been grown and filled with all sorts of plants associated with the Mother of God.

Prayers for the Day

Prayer Taught to the Children at Fatima

Repeat 3 Times
My God, I believe, I adore, I hope, I love thee.
I ask pardon for those who do not believe, nor adore, nor hope, nor love thee.

Hail Mary

Repeat 10 times
Hail Mary, full of grace,
the Lord is with thee.
Blessed are thou among women,
and blessed is the fruit of thy womb, Jesus.

Holy Mary, Mother of God,
pray for us sinners now,
and at the hour of our death.
Amen.

Pride and Humility

There are many examples of pride in our world. Pride seems to be at the heart of every problem. We can see it alive and well in *Green Eggs and Ham* by Dr. Seuss, where a character is convinced that he does not like green eggs and ham even though Sam-I-Am is trying to tell him how wonderful they are. He simply refuses to eat them. "I will not eat them, Sam-I-Am, I will not eat them with a goat," and so on.

Eventually, after being offered green eggs and ham in more variations than he ever dreamed possible, Sam-I-Am wears him down, so he finally tries the dish. And what does he find? He finds that he actually likes green eggs and ham! Just think of the amount of trouble that could have been saved if the new fan of green eggs and ham hadn't been so insistent about not liking the unusual dish.

Another example of pride is in *The Emperor's New Clothes* by Hans Christian Anderson. Two robbers show up promising the most wonderful new clothes for the fashionable emperor. They promise to provide impressive outfits, but there is a small twist. Only those who are very clever, or are qualified for the position they hold in the emperor's court, will be able to see the luxurious cloth.

After days of pretending to be weaving, when they really were stealing the emperor's treasures, the thieves are visited by one of the emperor's representatives. He spends some time observing the weavers as they work, but he cannot see a single thread. Afraid that he will appear ignorant or not qualified for his position, he praises the robbers on their beautiful cloth and shares his glowing report with the emperor and the rest of the staff.

A few days later, after the thieves have collected huge amounts of silk and golden thread and loads of gold coins, they announce that it is time for the emperor to dress in the remarkable clothes. All the emperor's men come to help him dress and prepare for a parade in the fine new clothes. This is how it goes for some time—everyone pretending to see what really isn't there—until finally someone with nothing to lose pipes up. It is a child who says, "But the Emperor has nothing on at all!" With that, everyone is then free to say what they had been thinking the whole time: the emperor has nothing on! It was pride—for fear of looking like they weren't smart or that they didn't deserve their positions—that caused everyone else to remain silent.

Pride can deceive us. It can make us think that we are the most important person on earth, or in the case of the emperor, that we must not look like a fool and tell the truth. The opposite virtue is humility. It is the ability to stay little and childlike, saying what is true, like the little child who finally told the truth about the emperor's clothes (or lack of clothes). Humility also helps us have a pure heart. Jesus once said, "Blessed are the clean of heart, for they will see God" (Mt 5:8). Why? Because when we are full of pride, we think of ourselves first and don't see how we fit into the world in the right way.

No one has seen God quite the way that our Blessed Mother has. How do we know this? Because she has the purest heart of all. In her selflessness, her humility, and her purity, her vision of God is the clearest out of every human creature.

Discussion Questions

1. Why did the people around the emperor play into the lie about his clothes?

2. Can you think of other examples where pride blinded someone to the truth?

3. Why does humility give us the ability to see God?

Did You Know?

Ladybugs are named for Mary. In the icons of the Byzantine tradition, the Virgin is often depicted wearing red. The harmless red ladybug was named after her, particularly because the most common type that are found in Europe also have seven black spots, which are said to represent Mary's seven joys and sorrows. Legend has it that English farmers, overwhelmed by pests in their crops, prayed to Our Lady. Soon after, ladybugs arrived, eating the pests while leaving the crops alone. The farmers gave them the name "Our Lady's beetle", which stuck in some places and was also adopted in other European languages.

Prayers for the Day

Prayer Taught to the Children at Fatima

Repeat 3 Times
My God, I believe, I adore, I hope, I love thee.
I ask pardon for those who do not believe, nor adore, nor hope, nor love thee.

Hail Mary

Repeat 10 times
Hail Mary, full of grace,
the Lord is with thee.
Blessed are thou among women,
and blessed is the fruit of thy womb, Jesus.

Holy Mary, Mother of God,
pray for us sinners now,
and at the hour of our death.
Amen.

Envy and Kindness

Jealousy and envy are two words that we often use for the same thing, but they actually mean different things. Jealousy is that strong feeling we have when we want what someone else has, or when something we have is threatened by someone else. The focus of jealousy is an object that we want.

Envy, on the other hand, is directed at a person and not a thing. Envy is that feeling we have when someone gets what we want and we hate him or her for it because we see it as a lessening of who we are. In addition to anger, it can also be experienced as sorrow or spite. The key is that I don't just want what someone else has, I want to destroy it, either by destroying the person, the good thing, or both. Envy, rather than being happy for someone because of a good thing in his life, turns into resentment, spite, and malice.

The timeless tale of *Cinderella* has been told many ways over thousands of years and across many cultures. Although some of the story's details change, one that seems to be in most of the Cinderella-type stories is the mean stepmother and stepsisters. They hate Cinderella because she is good and beautiful and they are not. Unable to get rid of her, they do the next best thing and make her their slave. They treat her very poorly, feed her very little, make her work night and day, and never consider any kind of a future for her beyond serving them.

Sleeping Beauty and *Snow White* are other examples of this, where the wicked witch doesn't want to compete with the princess's beauty, so she casts a spell upon her that will last for one hundred years. With the young beauty out of the way, the witch wants to reclaim her title of "fairest of them all." As we have seen with the other vices, envy destroys our souls because the poison of desiring to destroy the life or good of another is never a healthy thing.

The opposite virtue of envy is a blend of kindness, charity, and humility where we feel pleased that good things are happening to others, no matter how it may affect our lives. When we know that God has his own plan for our lives, we are free to rejoice in the good things that happen to others instead of allowing them to ruin us.

Although she truly is "the fairest of them all," Our Lady lives out charity and humility, which makes her quite different from the witches and goddesses we read about in old fairy tales. In her trust, she offers us a model to be content with the good things God gives us and to rejoice in the good that comes to others.

Discussion Questions

1. Have you ever felt envious of someone else?

2. How did it make you feel inside?

3. How does being grateful help you to overcome envy?

Did You Know?

There are over 150 well-known music composers throughout history, such as Mozart and Bach. Out of all of these, 117 master composers wrote pieces of music about or dedicated to Our Lady, covering all of her joys and sorrows as the Mother of God. There are also a remarkable number of hymns, liturgies, and poetry written for Mary, such as the Regina Caeli, Salve Regina, Ave Maria, and the Stabbat Mater.

Prayers for the Day

Prayer Taught to the Children at Fatima

Repeat 3 Times
My God, I believe, I adore, I hope, I love thee.
I ask pardon for those who do not believe,
nor adore, nor hope, nor love thee.

Hail Mary

Repeat 10 times
Hail Mary, full of grace,
the Lord is with thee.
Blessed are thou among women,
and blessed is the fruit of thy womb, Jesus.

Holy Mary, Mother of God,
pray for us sinners now,
and at the hour of our death.
Amen.

Anger and Meekness

In the story of *Anne of Green Gables*, Gilbert Blythe teasingly calls Anne Shirley "carrots" because of her red hair. Anne, who is *very* sensitive about having red hair, becomes so angry that she takes her school slate (like a little chalk board) and smashes it on Gilbert's head.

Of course, Anne gets in a lot of trouble for this. Even though she said she was sorry, it takes Anne a long time to forgive Gilbert and accept him as a friend. She says she could never forgive him for calling her carrots and holds a deep grudge against him for many years. Ironically, despite all the years of anger, Anne and Gilbert eventually got married. Through forgiveness, the anger was forgotten and something new and beautiful was able to develop.

I think we can all relate to the idea of getting really angry with someone. There is always going to be a struggle when people come together with different characters, motivations, weaknesses, and interests. But what makes our action a vice or a virtue is how we respond. Do we respond like Anne Shirley and break the nearest thing around over the head of the one who made us angry? Or do we try to control our emotions and act in a way that won't make the situation worse? Anger as a vice is when we make the situation worse because our emotions are out of control, like when we yell back at that brother who has just yelled at us, or when we hit someone because we don't like what she said.

Meekness is the opposite of anger. Some people think that meekness means being weak or boring. But we know that the most powerful

God-man, Jesus, was the epitome of meekness. He didn't let his emotions get the best of him. Jesus was meek precisely because he had the power to change the circumstances but didn't because he knew everything that happened to him was part of God's will for his life. Mary, meanwhile, shows us her meekness because she followed her son, suffering along with him, and remained united to God's will instead of trying to stop it or complain about it.

So meekness isn't a sign of weakness; it's a sign that we are in control of our emotions and our will, while anger is a sign that our emotions and will are out of control. Often, our emotions can be like a wild horse and it is meekness that tames them.

There is such a thing as righteous anger, and that is when we see an injustice done to someone or to something that is good and sacred. Even in our righteous anger, though, we are called to be patient, prayerful, creative, and diligent in trying to correct the many wrongs we see in our world. It is an ancient Christian principle that we can never use a bad thing to try to make something good. In other words, we cannot use evil ways to try to get something good. We must use good actions to acquire good things.

Discussion Questions

1. Have you ever been so angry with someone you thought you could never forgive them?

2. What happens when we forgive someone? To them? To us?

3. What do people usually think meekness is? What is it really?

Did You Know?

Perhaps you have seen or even visited Notre Dame Cathedral in Paris, France. It is made in the Gothic style of architecture that was popular from roughly the twelfth through the sixteenth centuries. Much of the inspiration for this style came from the Virgin Mary. During this time, master builders were motivated to make a fitting church on earth for the Queen of Heaven. Several of the best-known Gothic churches are named Notre Dame, meaning "Our Lady", particularly those in the French cities of Paris, Chartres, and Reims.

Prayers for the Day

Prayer Taught to the Children at Fatima

Repeat 3 Times
My God, I believe, I adore, I hope, I love thee.
I ask pardon for those who do not believe, nor adore, nor hope, nor love thee.

Hail Mary

Repeat 10 times
Hail Mary, full of grace,
the Lord is with thee.
Blessed are thou among women,
and blessed is the fruit of thy womb, Jesus.

Holy Mary, Mother of God,
pray for us sinners now,
and at the hour of our death.
Amen.

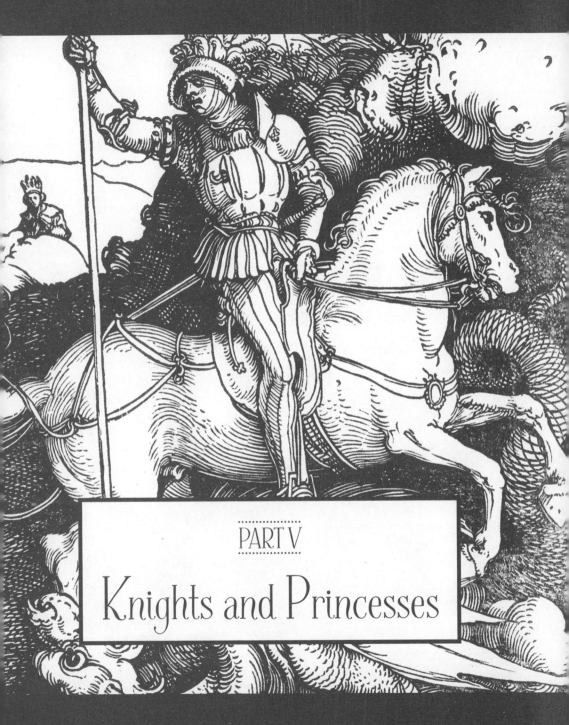

PART V

Knights and Princesses

Mary and Chivalry

Children's stories have long been filled with knights and princesses. There is something about the bravery of knights and the goodness and beauty of princesses that captures the hearts and minds of boys and girls everywhere. But princesses and knights are most interesting when they are engaged in some kind of a quest, or a struggle that involves the triumph of good over evil. We are drawn to such stories because, whether we know it or not, we are all involved in a great battle of good against evil.

It begins in the first book of the Bible, Genesis. After Adam and Eve disobey God and eat of the tree, enmity, or hatred, is put between the woman, who is Mary, and the serpent, who is the devil. God says to the serpent, "I will put enmity between you and the woman, and between your offspring and hers" (Gn 3:15).

There are many tales of great armies, heroic battles, and unstoppable leaders throughout history, but what is it about the medieval period, when there were knights and princesses fighting against dark forces, that is so interesting?

Perhaps it is because they are trying to follow Christ. In battles from different periods, it's hard to find good men because often the soldiers on both sides are motivated by the wrong things, such as power, money, or greed. But in most medieval stories, the heroes and heroines were motivated by something much nobler; often they did it for God, the preservation of civilization, and for Our Lady. They had a sense of a quest that brought a different kind of spirit to their efforts, and a new set of rules to their fighting, known as chivalry.

Chivalry was a code used by men during the age of knights, jousting, and suits of armor. The name comes from the French word for knight, *chevalier*. The good men of the time, influenced by the example of Jesus and many holy monks and priests, developed chivalry so that they would know how to act in accord with Christian teaching, even in the heat of battle or the fog of war. Chivalry provides the rules to help men choose the right way of being a warrior.

Another interesting characteristic of the age of chivalry was that Mary served as an important model for men and women. For women, she was the model of how to behave, while for men, how she was treated was the model for how all women ought to be treated.

This was something new. Christ brought a new idea to the world that women and men, although different, are actually equal in his sight. In Scripture, we see many times when Christ favored women, even though traditionally and in most all other cultures women have been treated as second-class citizens. But Christ changed that. We see examples of it at key moments in his life. For example, a woman, Our Lady, was the first to know when Jesus became incarnate, and likewise, it was a woman, Mary Magdalene, who was the first to see Christ after his resurrection.

As Christianity grew and spread, and as more people came to understand the importance of Mary, her influence upon culture and civilization grew quickly. Since Christ loved and honored his mother, he offered men who were normally rough brutes a new way to approach the Mother of God and, by extension, every woman. Christ and Mary were at the heart of what it meant to live the chivalrous code.

This week, we are going to look at the roles played by brave knights and good princesses, as well as other important tools we will need for our own quest. While it may not always feel like we are in midst of a huge battle, we are. You have an important role to play. Time to suit up!

Discussion Questions

1. What sorts of temptations do you think soldiers experience when in battle?

2. Why did chivalry help them with these temptations?

3. How did Mary help the code of chivalry?

Did You Know?

On a mountain in Italy called Montesiepi there sits a small round chapel. Within it is a glass case that houses a sword stuck deep in solid rock. In the twelfth century, a fierce and wealthy knight named Galgano converted to Catholicism after a visit from St. Michael the Archangel. According to legend, Galgano then heard a voice telling him to give up all of his riches and worldly desires. His reply was that it would be easier to split a stone with his sword than to give these things up. Drawing his sword, he tried to demonstrate his point, but to his amazement, as he struck the stone, the blade cut through it easily, and there his sword remains to this day. Clearly, the lesson of the sword in the stone stuck, because now the knight is known to us as Saint Galgano. This story is also similar to the sword in the stone tale of King Arthur, who was raised as an inconsequential orphan even though he was born with noble blood. A sword was lodged in a stone and only the man fit to rule England would be able to pull it from the stone slab. Many a man tried and many a man failed, until the humble but wise Arthur tried. As he pulled, the sword loosened and then came out clean. The crowd cheered and he was made king of England.

Prayers for the Day

The Apostles' Creed

I believe in God, the Father Almighty, Creator of heaven and earth;
and in Jesus Christ, his only Son, our Lord;
who was conceived by the Holy Spirit, born of the Virgin Mary,
suffered under Pontius Pilate, was crucified, died, and was buried.
He descended into hell; the third day he arose again from the dead.
He ascended into heaven, and sits at the right hand of God, the Father
   Almighty;
from thence he shall come to judge the living and the dead.
I believe in the Holy Spirit, the Holy Catholic Church,
the communion of saints, the forgiveness of sins,
the resurrection of the body and life everlasting.
Amen.

Our Father

Our Father,
who art in heaven,
hallowed be thy name;
thy kingdom come,
thy will be done,
on earth as it is in heaven.
Give us this day our daily bread,
and forgive us our trespasses,
as we forgive those who trespass against us;
and lead us not into temptation,
but deliver us from evil.
Amen.

Hail Mary

Repeat 10 times
Hail Mary, full of grace,
the Lord is with thee.
Blessed are thou among women,
and blessed is the fruit of thy womb, Jesus.

Holy Mary, Mother of God,
pray for us sinners now,
and at the hour of our death.
Amen.

Glory Be

Glory be to the Father,
to the Son,
and to the Holy Spirit,
as it was in the beginning,
is now, and ever shall be,
world without end.
Amen.

The Fatima Prayer

O my Jesus, forgive us our sins,
save us from the fires of hell,
and lead all souls to heaven,
especially those in most
need of your mercy.

What Is a Holy Knight?

Knighthood was a noble profession for many centuries. A boy training to be a knight started at age seven, and it took fourteen years for him to earn his knighthood. It involved lots of serious games and sports—many done on horseback—to acquire all the skills necessary for success in battle.

As we saw yesterday, chivalry helped people answer the question, "How can a man be a warrior and not lose his soul?" Becoming a knight wasn't just a hobby; it was vital to communities. There were often invaders looking for food, gold, or property, so it was important for cities to have a good defense. These physical battles were also seen in spiritual ways, like our own battles against temptation and vice. Books like *The Chronicles of Narnia* and *The Lord of the Rings* show us that physical and spiritual battles can be very much intertwined.

Jesus offered a different way to look at humanity. Prior to Christianity, power and domination were considered two of the highest virtues. Jesus, however, championed meekness, self-sacrifice, courage, bravery, and trust in the one true God. The sword, like Jesus, becomes not just a sign of power but a symbol of victory over sin and death. Even the Holy Grail, the cup used during the Last

Supper that many of the knights sought after, is a symbol of Christ and his outpouring of himself for us.

Perhaps one of the most famous knights is St. George. As legend has it, there was a town next to a lake, and in the lake was an island where a deadly dragon lived. The dragon continually attacked and ravaged the town's population. In order to stop the dragon from destroying the town, the people started feeding it sheep. And when they ran out of sheep, they started feeding it their children by lottery.

This all went on until one day when the king's daughter, the princess, was selected to be fed to the dragon. The king offered the town all of his gold and silver and half of his lands if his daughter could be spared. But they refused. The princess, dressed as a bride, was nearly to the boat when St. George happened upon the scene.

Making the sign of the cross, George knew he could help the young woman. As they spoke, the dragon came out of the water. George charged the beast with his lance, seriously wounding it. He then convinced the girl to throw her girdle around the dragon's neck, and when she did, the dragon became as docile and gentle as a puppy, following the girl wherever she led.

St. George addressed the people, saying, "If you all become Christians, I will kill the dragon for you." And sure enough, fifteen thousand people converted to Christianity and St. George killed the dragon. The king, in his relief at having his daughter spared, had a church built in honor of Our Lady and St. George at the place where the dragon died, and from this church flowed a spring of healing water that was a blessing to the town for all its days.

St. George is a great knight because he displayed courage, creativity, faith, charity, and evangelical zeal. He wanted to see the evil dragon destroyed and the people built up with faith. These are the set of ideas that have changed the world dramatically and have inspired so many to do the same. Mary, as the helper of Christians, defender of the faith, and mother to all, was at the heart of these ideas. She was inspiring, encouraging, and an aid to all who called upon her.

Discussion Questions

1. What sort of dangers do you think knights had to face?

2. What is the purpose of chivalry?

3. What makes a good knight?

Did You Know?

We don't witness wars and battles like they used to a long time ago, but the game of football is pretty close to warfare. Even in football, Mary has an important place: the Hail Mary pass. The desperation play was popularized during the 1975 game between the Dallas Cowboys and the Minnesota Vikings when Drew Pearson caught a game-winning pass. After the game, the Cowboy's quarterback, Roger Staubach—a Catholic—said, "I closed my eyes and said a Hail Mary." Previously, the term had only been used at

Notre Dame and other Catholic universities. The Hail Mary is technically always a long shot, but when it works, it is truly a cause of celebration by the winning team (as the losing team looks on helpless and stunned).

Prayers for the Day

The Apostles' Creed

I believe in God, the Father Almighty, Creator of heaven and earth;
and in Jesus Christ, his only Son, our Lord;
who was conceived by the Holy Spirit, born of the Virgin Mary,
suffered under Pontius Pilate, was crucified, died, and was buried.
He descended into hell; the third day he arose again from the dead.
He ascended into heaven, and sits at the right hand of God, the Father
    Almighty;
from thence he shall come to judge the living and the dead.
I believe in the Holy Spirit, the Holy Catholic Church,
the communion of saints, the forgiveness of sins,
the resurrection of the body and life everlasting.
Amen.

Our Father

Our Father,
who art in heaven,
hallowed be thy name;
thy kingdom come,
thy will be done,
on earth as it is in heaven.
Give us this day our daily bread,
and forgive us our trespasses,
as we forgive those who trespass against us;
and lead us not into temptation,
but deliver us from evil.
Amen.

Hail Mary

Repeat 10 times
Hail Mary, full of grace,
the Lord is with thee.
Blessed are thou among women,
and blessed is the fruit of thy womb, Jesus.

Holy Mary, Mother of God,
pray for us sinners now,
and at the hour of our death.
Amen.

Glory Be

Glory be to the Father,
to the Son,
and to the Holy Spirit,
as it was in the beginning,
is now, and ever shall be,
world without end.
Amen.

The Fatima Prayer

O my Jesus, forgive us our sins, save us from the fires of hell, and lead all souls to heaven, especially those in most need of your mercy.

What's So Special About Princesses?

Princesses are an important part of storytelling and have been for a very long time. There are some basic ideas that make up every good princess story, but most often the story is about a princess who is targeted by another woman, usually a queen, who is jealous of her beauty and goodness. In the end, the bad queen is defeated, freeing the good princess to live freely with her prince and rule her lands happily.

While we know these stories well, we don't often think about what makes the bad queen bad and the good princess good. One of the vices we discussed last week was envy. In princess tales, the bad queen is envious of the princess. She knows she is not as beautiful or as good as the princess is and wants her to be destroyed so she can be "the fairest of them all." We see this same pattern in *Snow White*, *Sleeping Beauty*, *The Little Mermaid*, and *Cinderella*.

So what is it, then, that we like about good princesses? It's easy to think they are good simply because they're beautiful princesses with wealth and servants, but if a princess is spoiled by such things, she will not be the good princess of a story; actually, if she does become spoiled, she will soon find herself becoming the story's bad queen.

There was a book written about seven hundred years ago by a woman, Christine de Pizan, who lived amongst a lot of princesses. She warned young women not to believe they were the most important person around. She cautioned against always trying to amuse themselves, spending too much time on their jewelry and clothing, and treating everyone as if they existed only to serve her.

Christine saw a lot of princesses fall into bad habits, so she wrote a book to offer advice about how to be a good princess. In her book, the most important thing Christine warned princesses against was becoming filled with pride—whether it was pride in their beauty, opinions, or authority. She suggested the best way to avoid pride is to always remember that everything we have and everything we are comes from God. Humility, then, is the most important virtue a princess—or any woman, man, and child—can work toward. Another holy writer has pointed out that in heaven there are many people with different vocations and beautiful qualities, but what all of them have in common is that they are humble. Humility is the most important virtue we need to get to heaven, so the more we can remember that God has given us every gift we have, the easier it will be to become holy.

The best example of a queen is of course Mary, who is called the Queen of Heaven and Earth. She is the humblest even though, or maybe because, she is so exalted by God. She knows everything she has is from him and not of her own making. Mary is never focused on herself or on unimportant things. The best princesses are those who model themselves after Mary's example.

Discussion Questions

1. What makes bad queens so bad in the stories you are familiar with?

2. What do we like about good princesses?

3. What vices can turn a good princess into a bad queen?

Did You Know?

In every apparition of the Virgin Mary, the people who saw her said, "I saw the most beautiful woman I have ever seen." Mary's beauty was always something that moved them to love her and to become better Christians. Even St. Therese had an experience of Our Lady's beauty when she was suffering greatly as a child. Little Therese turned to a statue of Mary near her bed and begged Mary to have pity upon her through the terrible suffering. She writes, "All of a sudden, the statue became alive! The Virgin became beautiful, so beautiful that I could never find words to express it. . . . But what penetrated to the roots of my being was her ravishing smile. At that moment, all my pains vanished." Mary's beauty isn't beauty for its own sake, but it points to the goodness of God.

Prayers for the Day

The Apostles' Creed

I believe in God, the Father Almighty, Creator of heaven and earth;
and in Jesus Christ, his only Son, our Lord;
who was conceived by the Holy Spirit, born of the Virgin Mary,
suffered under Pontius Pilate, was crucified, died, and was buried.
He descended into hell; the third day he arose again from the dead.

He ascended into heaven, and sits at the right hand of God, the Father
    Almighty;
from thence he shall come to judge the living and the dead.
I believe in the Holy Spirit, the Holy Catholic Church,
the communion of saints, the forgiveness of sins,
the resurrection of the body and life everlasting.
Amen.

Our Father

Our Father,
who art in heaven,
hallowed be thy name;
thy kingdom come,
thy will be done,
on earth as it is in heaven.
Give us this day our daily bread,
and forgive us our trespasses,
as we forgive those who trespass against us;
and lead us not into temptation,
but deliver us from evil.
Amen.

Hail Mary

Repeat 10 times
Hail Mary, full of grace,
the Lord is with thee.
Blessed are thou among women,
and blessed is the fruit of thy womb, Jesus.

Holy Mary, Mother of God,
pray for us sinners now,
and at the hour of our death.
Amen.

Glory Be

Glory be to the Father,
to the Son,
and to the Holy Spirit,
as it was in the beginning,
is now, and ever shall be,
world without end.
Amen.

The Fatima Prayer

O my Jesus, forgive us our sins, save us from the fires of hell, and lead all souls to heaven, especially those in most need of your mercy.

Beauty and Brawn

Sometimes in our culture it can be hard to see the distinct gifts that men and women have and how they can be used together. God made men and women to be complementary, which means that the gifts men have work in harmony with the gifts women have, and *vice versa.*

Together, when a man and a woman are called to marriage, they are much stronger than they ever could be as individuals. Fairy tales and chivalry remind us of how important these gifts can be, especially when the world is full of strife and struggle. During such times, couples, families, and communities come together to take care of everyone's needs.

During the age of chivalry, men were valued for their strength and women for their beauty. If that was all we knew about this stage of history, we would think that it was a very shallow way to look at humanity. But we know that beauty and brawn were not just valued because of vanity or pride but because they were also seen in a deeper light. For men, strength was important because it allowed them to protect their families and communities. But strength had to be accompanied by many other virtues for it to be considered a noble quality. There is nothing good about a man who shows off his strength just to show he is strong. Yet there is something wonderful about the soldier who knows when and how to use his strength for good.

It's also interesting to note the significant role that Mary played in the lives of many Christian soldiers. They kept her very close, particularly in battle. Mary was both their inspiration and their intercessor, helping them at every turn. During the twelfth century, one knight wrote, **"Our Lady is powerful in battles, she is the hope of . . . knights who fight. . . . Without her aid, knights cannot win."**

A significant part of Mary's influence was her beauty coupled with her goodness. She was the model of womanhood since God made her to be the perfect woman. While beautiful women never go out of style, Christian cultures understood that the beauty of Mary, as well as the beauty of everyday

women, all point to the same source: to the beauty of God. What we often miss is that girls and women spend a lot of time trying to be beautiful, but why? Many do it for reasons of vanity, but the desire in their hearts is for something much deeper. Sadly, a lot of women then (and now) thought that being the most beautiful woman in the land would make them happy, but we see over and over again that beauty is often only skin deep and is not what brings about true happiness. True happiness resides in beauty that lives virtuously and is coupled with goodness. It was the beauty of the princess's soul that inspired knights to protect them.

We may laugh off beauty and brawn as values from long ago, but we still have to ask: why do we love these princess and knight stories so much? And why do women desire still to be beautiful? And men to be strong? Because God put these gifts in our hearts—he wants his kind of beauty and strength to be seen in the world.

Discussion Questions

1. How do you think the beauty of women can be used for good?

2. Can you think of ways that the strength of men can be used for good?

3. How do you think these gifts can work together to make a couple stronger than if they were used alone?

Did You Know?

The feast of Our Lady of the Rosary was originally called the feast of Our Lady of Victory. The feast came about after the Holy League, which was made up of the pope and countries like Spain and Italy along the Mediterranean Sea, fought a great naval battle against the Turks called the Battle of Lepanto. Pope Pius V and all the soldiers prayed the Rosary before the battle, knowing they were outnumbered in might and men. When the battle came, again through Mary's miraculous intercession, the wind shifted, dramatically tipping victory to the hands of the Christians and saving Europe from an even greater Muslim invasion.

Prayers for the Day

The Apostles' Creed

I believe in God, the Father Almighty, Creator of heaven and earth;
and in Jesus Christ, his only Son, our Lord;
who was conceived by the Holy Spirit, born of the Virgin Mary,
suffered under Pontius Pilate, was crucified, died, and was buried.
He descended into hell; the third day he arose again from the dead.
He ascended into heaven, and sits at the right hand of God, the Father
   Almighty;
from thence he shall come to judge the living and the dead.
I believe in the Holy Spirit, the Holy Catholic Church,
the communion of saints, the forgiveness of sins,
the resurrection of the body and life everlasting.
Amen.

Our Father

Our Father,
who art in heaven,
hallowed be thy name;
thy kingdom come,
thy will be done,
on earth as it is in heaven.
Give us this day our daily bread,
and forgive us our trespasses,
as we forgive those who trespass against us;
and lead us not into temptation,

but deliver us from evil.
Amen.

Hail Mary

Repeat 10 times
Hail Mary, full of grace,
the Lord is with thee.
Blessed are thou among women,
and blessed is the fruit of thy womb, Jesus.

Holy Mary, Mother of God,
pray for us sinners now,
and at the hour of our death.
Amen.

Glory Be

Glory be to the Father,
to the Son,
and to the Holy Spirit,
as it was in the beginning,
is now, and ever shall be,
world without end.
Amen.

The Fatima Prayer

O my Jesus, forgive us our sins, save us from the fires of hell, and lead all
souls to heaven, especially those in most need of your mercy.

DAY 31

Courage

Fear is something that everyone faces. It makes us want to hide and not do anything, or to pretend that a problem doesn't exist. For this reason, "Do not be afraid" is the most common phrase in the Bible. God knows that we are afraid, but he also knows that he and his mother are with us to help.

Courage, on the other hand, does not mean that someone acts without fear. Courage means that a person has said his prayers, knows what he must do, and trusts God through whatever may happen. Yes, there still might be fear, but the awareness and importance of what must be done overshadows that feeling.

In *The Lord of the Rings,* Frodo and Samwise have a task that seems impossible: to destroy the ring at Mordor. Every stage of their journey is fraught with something scary, chilling, unsettling, and threatening. And yet the two continue together on their journey.

Even the modern epic film *Star Wars* (the 1977 original) is modeled on the medieval model of knights, princesses, and an overwhelming evil that must be stopped before all good is overcome. Luke Skywalker, the "futuristic knight," must find the Death Star's weakest link so that it and Darth Vader can be overcome. The success of Luke and his fellow knights (the Jedi) are like a modern-day David and Goliath.

Courage isn't just for men. We see this virtue being lived out in the lives of many women throughout history, but particularly in the famous French knight Joan of Arc. Joan is one of those saints that God made once and hasn't replicated (as far as we know). As a child, she was tasked to help lead the French army against the invading English by none other than St. Michael the Archangel, St. Catherine of Siena, and St. Margaret, who appeared to her in a vision when she was a small child. Knowing it was time for her to fulfill her task, she petitioned military leaders to let her join the king in the fight.

"I must be at the king's side," Joan explained. "There will be no help (for the kingdom) if not from me. Although I would rather have remained spinning [wool] at my mother's side . . . yet must I go and must I do this thing, for my Lord wills that I do so."

Believing her advice to be divinely inspired, the French king, Charles VII, moved against the English according to her plans. Joan led the French army to a momentous victory over the English at the Battle of Orleans. She was eventually captured by the English, put on trial, and then burned at the stake. Throughout all of this, Joan said, "I am not afraid, I was born to do this." Clearly, she was a woman with supernatural courage who knew her mission.

When we understand that we have a mission, it is much easier to have courage. Mary showed this courage when the angel Gabriel appeared to her at the Annunciation. Although she did not understand all of the divine plans, she offered her "yes" to God without hesitation.

Discussion Questions

1. Why do you think we all feel afraid sometimes?

2. How can we find courage, even when we are afraid?

3. How can focusing on the mission God has given us in life help us to be courageous?

Did You Know?

Prince Eugene of Savoy (1663–1736) was the monarch and commander-in-chief who finally ended the Islamic occupations in Europe. Not just a spectator, the warrior prince was known to have fought with the Rosary in one hand and a sword in another. Any time his soldiers saw him praying the Rosary, they knew another battle was about to begin.

Prayers for the Day

The Apostles' Creed

I believe in God, the Father Almighty, Creator of heaven and earth;
and in Jesus Christ, his only Son, our Lord;
who was conceived by the Holy Spirit, born of the Virgin Mary,
suffered under Pontius Pilate, was crucified, died, and was buried.
He descended into hell; the third day he arose again from the dead.
He ascended into heaven, and sits at the right hand of God, the Father
Almighty;
from thence he shall come to judge the living and the dead.
I believe in the Holy Spirit, the Holy Catholic Church,
the communion of saints, the forgiveness of sins,
the resurrection of the body and life everlasting.
Amen.

Our Father

Our Father,
who art in heaven,
hallowed be thy name;
thy kingdom come,
thy will be done,
on earth as it is in heaven.
Give us this day our daily bread,
and forgive us our trespasses,
as we forgive those who trespass against us;
and lead us not into temptation,

but deliver us from evil.
Amen.

Hail Mary

Repeat 10 times
Hail Mary, full of grace,
the Lord is with thee.
Blessed are thou among women,
and blessed is the fruit of thy womb, Jesus.

Holy Mary, Mother of God,
pray for us sinners now,
and at the hour of our death.
Amen.

Glory Be

Glory be to the Father,
to the Son,
and to the Holy Spirit,
as it was in the beginning,
is now, and ever shall be,
world without end.
Amen.

The Fatima Prayer

O my Jesus, forgive us our sins, save us from the fires of hell, and lead all souls to heaven, especially those in most need of your mercy.

Faith

Whether it is chivalry, the saints, or trying to grow in virtue, all of our Christian endeavors require the virtue of faith. This is another gift we are given at baptism, but like the other virtues, it can wane or wax. What we do and the choices we make can help our faith grow strong or winnow it away into something that is barely there.

Scripture describes faith as "the realization of what is hoped for and evidence of things not seen" (Heb 11:1). It is a mysterious balance of what we have been given and something else we desire that hasn't arrived yet. St. Paul warns us that without faith, it is impossible to please God, "for anyone who approaches God must believe that he exists and that he rewards those who seek him" (Heb 11:6).

The Eucharist is one area that requires a lot of faith to appreciate it fully. We know that the Mass is the source and summit of our existence because it embodies Christ, but so many scarcely believe this because it looks just like another piece of bread. And yet it is worth much, much more.

In the book *The Weight of a Mass* by Josephine Nobisso, an old woman enters into a bustling bakery to beg for some stale bread. "If you will give me a crust of stale bread, I will offer my Mass tonight for you." But the baker scoffs, "Let God provide her bread!"

In order to mock the poor woman even more, he takes a small piece of tissue paper and writes "One Mass" on it. He then puts it on his scales to see what it might weigh (in an attempt to see what the Mass was worth). Of course, the baker assumed the tissue paper would weigh virtually nothing. But as he went about adding cakes, tarts, and cupcakes on the other side of the scale, the side with the Mass on it didn't budge. This confused the baker very much. He expected the Mass, the tissue paper, to rise high in the air opposite the weight of the food. So he added more. Still, the paper held down the weight.

After a few seconds lost in his confusion, the baker picked up the tiny piece of paper, and suddenly all the towering items fell to the ground. Confused even further, the baker then tested his scales to make sure they were not broken. They were fine. So he took the tiny piece of paper and put it back, but on the other side of the scale. Sure enough, as he stacked up item after item, the "One Mass" scrap would not budge. It weighed more than anything he put on the other side.

Across the street, a king was set to marry the future queen in a beautiful Mass, but everyone was too busy to partake in the Mass. They only cared about the celebration afterward, which the baker had baked an elegant cake for. He added this very cake to the stack on the opposite side of the piece of paper. Still again, the Mass weighed more than everything the baker could put on the scale.

By this time, quite a crowd had gathered. As they watched the event unfold, they slowly started to peel away from the group and head across the street to the church. Finally, the baker had nothing left to weigh against the Mass. He told the old woman to take what she wanted, and they all headed to the wedding Mass. He told the old woman, "Come every day. You will never go hungry again."

Blessed are those who are able to see such miracles occur, but even more blessed are those who believe without proof. Many times in our lives, we can feel a bit like the hungry old woman, believing something that no one else seems to see, and yet even she didn't know what a wonderful thing she had, for even she thought the Mass was only worth some stale bread. May we always remember it is worth much, much more than that, and if ever we forget, let us pray to our Blessed Mother in heaven, who will never fail to remind us how important the Mass and the Blessed Sacrament are.

Discussion Questions

1. Why is faith a difficult virtue to hold onto?

2. Why do you think the baker scoffed at the old woman?

3. Have you ever had the experience of telling the truth about something and people didn't believe you?

Did You Know?

In the military battles where Mary is invoked, there is a repeating pattern where a surprising advantage tips the scales. In battle after battle, there is a similar storyline: the Christians are outnumbered but they have done their spiritual homework; the fighting starts; and then out of the blue, something odd happens and the Christians are victorious. In the Battle of New Orleans during the War of 1812, General Andrew Jackson's army of six thousand faced fifteen thousand British. All the residents of the city of New Orleans joined the Ursuline nuns in praying to Our Lady of Prompt Succor. On the morning of the battle, at the end of Mass where the Ursuline nuns were praying, a courier came with the news that the Americans had won. The British, who had been counting on advancing under the cover of fog, were exposed and routed when the mist unexpectedly lifted.

Prayers for the Day

The Apostles' Creed

I believe in God, the Father Almighty, Creator of heaven and earth;
and in Jesus Christ, his only Son, our Lord;
who was conceived by the Holy Spirit, born of the Virgin Mary,
suffered under Pontius Pilate, was crucified, died, and was buried.
He descended into hell; the third day he arose again from the dead.
He ascended into heaven, and sits at the right hand of God, the Father
    Almighty;
from thence he shall come to judge the living and the dead.
I believe in the Holy Spirit, the Holy Catholic Church,

the communion of saints, the forgiveness of sins,
the resurrection of the body and life everlasting.
Amen.

Our Father

Our Father,
who art in heaven,
hallowed be thy name;
thy kingdom come,
thy will be done,
on earth as it is in heaven.
Give us this day our daily
bread,
and forgive us our trespasses,
as we forgive those who trespass against us;
and lead us not into temptation,
but deliver us from evil.
Amen.

Hail Mary

Repeat 10 times
Hail Mary, full of grace,
the Lord is with thee.
Blessed are thou among women,
and blessed is the fruit of thy womb, Jesus.

Holy Mary, Mother of God,
pray for us sinners now,
and at the hour of our death.
Amen.

Glory Be

Glory be to the Father,
to the Son,
and to the Holy Spirit,
as it was in the beginning,
is now, and ever shall be,
world without end.
Amen.

The Fatima Prayer

O my Jesus, forgive us our sins, save us from the fires of hell, and lead all souls to heaven, especially those in most need of your mercy.

Let Mary Be Your Guide

Over the last month, we have looked at many important things: Christ's love for us, the role that Mary plays in our lives as our mother, the young saints who have been close friends to Mary and Jesus, and the many ways we can come closer to them by growing in virtue and resisting vice.

Our life here on earth has a purpose, no matter what age you are. The Lord has given you a mission that only you can fulfill. But he doesn't leave everything to us; he provides all kinds of helpers along the way, from our parents and teachers to our friends and siblings and even our guardian angels. But perhaps the best helper God has given us is Mary. St. Bernard of Clairvaux (1090–1158) wrote this about her:

> "And the virgin's name was Mary" (Lk 1:27). Let us also say a few words about this name which means "star of the sea" and is most suitably fitting for a virgin mother. For she is most appropriately compared to a star, because, just as a star emits rays without being corrupted, so the Virgin gave birth to her Son without any injury.
>
> If you follow her, you will not go astray. If you pray to her, you will not despair. If you think of her, you will not be lost. If you cling to her, you will not fall. If she protects you, you will not fear; if she is your guide, you will not tire; if she is favorable to you, you will reach your goal. Thus you will

experience personally how rightly it was spoke: "And the virgin's name was Mary."

Mary is here to help us with every struggle that we face. Drawing closer to her through this consecration will only make her presence in your life more noticeable. She is your mother. She loves you very much and will help you with whatever happens in your life. If you let her, our loving mother will always lead you home to her Son in heaven.

Discussion Questions

1. What have you learned about Mary through this consecration?

2. Did you have a favorite part, story, or reflection?

3. In preparation for tomorrow's consecration, what are you most grateful for when it comes to having Mary in your life?

Did You Know?

When he was a young man, Pope Saint John Paul II consecrated himself to Mary. He called the consecration a turning point in his life. He came to understand that in loving Mary and adding devotion to her in his life, he was living out more fully the will of the Trinity. As pope, he referred to that consecration and his devotion to Mary in his motto, *Totus Tuus* ("Totally Yours"), and added an *M* to his papal crest for Mary. When he was shot on May 13, 1981, the anniversary of the Fatima apparitions, the pope believed firmly that one hand had pulled the trigger of the gun, while another hand, Mary's hand, guided the bullet, sparing his life.

Prayers for the Day

The Apostles' Creed

I believe in God, the Father Almighty, Creator of heaven and earth;
and in Jesus Christ, his only Son, our Lord;
who was conceived by the Holy Spirit, born of the Virgin Mary,
suffered under Pontius Pilate, was crucified, died, and was buried.
He descended into hell; the third day he arose again from the dead.
He ascended into heaven, and sits at the right hand of God, the Father Almighty;
from thence he shall come to judge the living and the dead.
I believe in the Holy Spirit, the Holy Catholic Church,
the communion of saints, the forgiveness of sins,
the resurrection of the body and life everlasting.
Amen.

Our Father

Our Father,
who art in heaven,
hallowed be thy name;
thy kingdom come,
thy will be done,
on earth as it is in heaven.
Give us this day our daily bread,
and forgive us our trespasses,
as we forgive those who trespass against us;
and lead us not into temptation,
but deliver us from evil.
Amen.

Hail Mary

Repeat 10 times
Hail Mary, full of grace,
the Lord is with thee.
Blessed are thou among women,
and blessed is the fruit of thy womb, Jesus.

Holy Mary, Mother of God,
pray for us sinners now,
and at the hour of our death.
Amen.

Glory Be

Glory be to the Father,
to the Son,
and to the Holy Spirit,
as it was in the beginning,
is now, and ever shall be,
world without end.
Amen.

The Fatima Prayer

O my Jesus, forgive us our sins, save us from the fires of hell, and lead all souls to heaven, especially those in most need of your mercy.

Act of Consecration

Today is the day! It is your special feast as you pray this prayer to complete your Marian consecration. You have prayed hard and learned much. Perhaps you can photocopy this page and put it in your Bible to refer to in the future and remind you of this important feast in your life.

To say your consecration prayer, set some time aside or perhaps go to a Church to offer yourself fully to Our Lady. Once you have done this, you have completed your consecration to Mary.

This is an adaptation of the original consecration prayer written by St. Louis de Montfort.

Dear Jesus and Mary,

I love you. I offer myself to you this day through the renewal of my baptismal promises, but also by giving everything to you. I know that you love me more than I can ever imagine and that you wish every good thing for my life.

Mary, I know that as the Mother of Jesus, you will bring me closer to him and as my mother, you will help me to become the person God intends for me to be. You will protect me, guide me, and love me through the good times of my life, but also through the difficult times in my life. You will protect me from the many traps set against me by the devil for my whole life.

In my desire to show my love for you, I offer you everything—my life, my actions, the rewards for any action of mine, my thoughts, my love. I know that as a human being, I can only offer to Jesus very small things but that you will take my little offerings and present them to him in a special way. Like the Queen Mother of previous ages, you know what your Son will like best and will find a way to make my small offerings something that will please him.

You are Mary, the Mother of God, the Queen of Heaven and Earth, the Star of the Sea, and so much more. Today, I _____, take you as my mother and ask you to always remember me as a devoted child. Never let me be far from you. Keep me. Bless me. Protect me. Teach me. Nourish me. Bring me to the Holy Trinity, today and at the hour of my death. Help me to love you and your Son more and more throughout my life. Fill in my weaknesses and give me your humility.

Thank you for receiving this little offering from me, Mary, my mother.

Amen.

Sign Name Here:

_____

Date:

_____

Living Out Your Marian Consecration

There are many ways we can continue to honor Our Lady throughout the year to increase our relationship with our spiritual mother. Here are a few suggestions.

Renew Your Consecration Every Year

Now that you have made the Marian consecration, you can renew it again each year either by doing the thirty-three-day preparation again, or just saying the prayer of consecration on your consecration anniversary.

Pray a Daily Rosary

You may already know how to pray the Rosary, which is fantastic. If you don't know it, however, you learned all of the prayers necessary to pray the Rosary through this consecration. You may not have memorized them, but at least you are familiar with them. Ask a parent to teach you how to pray it, or learn it together. There is something very powerful about praying the Rosary as a family. It will bring many graces and beautiful blessings to the whole family. But if you can't pray it together, praying it on your own is a wonderful way to continue growing closer to Jesus and Mary.

Learn Marian Hymns

There are many beautiful Marian hymns that help us show our love for Our Lady, such as the Salve Regina, Immaculate Mary, and the Ave Maria. Perhaps you already know these. See if you can find other hymns to teach to your friends and family.

Say a Hail Mary When You Hear Sirens

When I was young, a dear woman taught me and my brother to say a Hail Mary whenever we heard a siren. Years later, he and I realized that we still did it. Mrs. Meier made quite the impression on us. I do it with my children now, and often they will be the ones to suggest it even before I do. It is a wonderful habit to pray for those who we know are in need.

Celebrate Marian Feasts

The year is full of Marian feasts, beginning with the feast of Mary, the Mother of God on January 1 and continuing all the way through to the feast of Our Lady of Guadalupe on December 12, with plenty more in between. There are many ways to celebrate these feasts: by going to Mass, praying the Rosary, or sharing a special meal or treat with your family. For example, for the feast of Mary as Queen of Heaven and Earth on August 22, you could make star cookies in honor of the "woman clothed with the sun, with the moon under her feet, and on her head a crown of twelve stars" (Rv 12:1). Or you could make her a birthday cake on her birthday, which the Church celebrates on September 8.

Tell Stories of Miracles

Reading stories about the saints and about Mary's life and the miracles performed through her intercession is always a wonderful way to get to know God better and how it is that he works through the saints.

Plant a Mary Garden

There are so many flowers and plants named after Mary that huge gardens have been planted in her honor. This can be done on a grand scale, covering many acres, or just in a small patch in your yard. Whatever beauty you offer to Mary, she will love!

Make Your Own Rosaries

There are many ways to make rosaries, either with beads or tying cord into knots. It is a joy to be able to share the Rosary with others through handmade rosaries that feature your favorite saints and devotions.

Marian Art

It is easier to stay close to Mary if we have reminders about her in our home. Some people like to put statues in their living rooms and pray around them at prayer time, while others like to have statues of her in their yards and give her a crown of flowers during her month of May. Icons, paintings, or even your own artwork honoring Our Lady are wonderful things to keep around you at home.

Wear a Commemorative Bracelet or Piece of Jewelry

St. Louis de Montfort suggests that those who have gone through the Marian Consecration wear some sort of chain around their wrist or ankle as a reminder of the Marian Consecration. Others have worn rings or necklaces to honor the festive event in their lives, which can serve as a visible reminder of your devotion to Mary and her love for you.

SOURCES

Books

Anderson, Hans Christian. *The Emperor's New Clothes.* Illustrated by Virginia Lee Burton. Boston: Houghton Mifflin, 1977.

Brown, Marcia, trans. *Cinderella.* New York: Aladdin Books, 1982.

Brown, Margaret Wise. *The Runaway Bunny.* Illustrated by Clement Hurd. New York: Harper and Row, 1972.

Burnett, Frances Hodgson. *Little Lord Fauntleroy.* New York: Puffin Classics, 2011.

Dahl, Ronald. *Charlie and the Chocolate Factory.* New York: Alfred Knopf, 1964.

de Montfort, Louis. *True Devotion to Mary.* Charlotte, NC: TAN Books, 2010.

Dr. Seuss. *Green Eggs and Ham.* New York: Beginner Books, 1960.

Gambero, Luigi. *Mary in the Middle Ages.* San Francisco: Ignatius Press, 2005.

Lewis, C. S. *The Chronicles of Narnia, Books 1-7.* Illustrated by Pauline Baynes. New York: Hare Collins Publishers, 1978.

The Little Red Hen. Illustrated by Lucinda McQueen. New York: Scholastic, 1985.

McBratney, Sam. *Guess How Much I Love You.* Illustrated by Anita Jeram. Candlewick Press, 2008.

Milne, A. A. *The Complete Tales of Winnie the Pooh.* New York: Dutton Children's Books, 1956.

Montgomery, L. M. *Anne of Green Gables.* London: Macmillan Collector's Library, 2014.

Nobisso, Josephine. *Take it to the Queen* Illustrated by Katalin Szegedi. Westhampton Beach, NY: Gingerbread House, 2008.

———. *The Weight of the Mass.* Illustrated by Katlin Szegedi. Westhampton Beach, NY: Gingerbread House, 2002.

Palmer, Helen. *A Fish Out of Water.* Illustrator P. D. Eastman. New York: Beginner Books, 1961.

Pernoud, Régine. *Joan of Arc By Herself and Her Witnesses.* Lanham, MD: Scarborough House, 1982.

Remensnyder, Amy G. *La Conquistadora.* London: Oxford University Press, 2014.

St. Therese of the Child Jesus and the Holy Face. *The Story a Soul.* Translated by Michael Day. Rockford, IL: TAN Books, 1997.

Tolkein, J. R. R. *The Lord of the Rings.* New York: Harper Collins, 2012.

Wojciechowski, Susan. *The Christmas Miracle of Jonathan Toomey.* Illustrated by P. J. Lynch. Somerville, MA: Candlewick Press, 2015.

Articles and Blogs

Bereit, Margaret. *Margaret Bereit* (blog). http://margaretbereit.com/.

Filz, Gretchen. "What Happened to Francisco & Jacinta Marto After Fatima." *Get Fed* (blog). The Catholic Company, February 20, 2017. https://www.catholiccompany.com/getfed/francisco-jacinta-marto-after-fatima/.

Hardon, John A. "Devotion of St. Therese of Lisieux to the Blessed Virgin Mary." The Real Presence Association. http://www.therealpresence.org/archives/Saints/Saints_027.htm.

Hines, Stephen. "'Mother, A Magic Word' By Laura Ingalls Wilder." *Little House on the Prairie* (blog). Friendly Family Productions. http://littlehouseontheprairie.com/mother-a-magic-word-by-laura-ingalls-wilder/.

Holloway, April. "Ten Legendary Swords from the Ancient World." *Ancient Origins,* July 1, 2015. http://www.ancient-origins.net/artifacts-other-artifacts/ten-legendary-swords-ancient-world-003335.

Kosloski, Philip. "An ancient Irish litany to the Blessed Virgin Mary." *Aleteia,* August 21, 2017. https://aleteia.org/2017/08/21/an-ancient-irish-litany-to-the-blessed-virgin-mary/.

———. "The oldest known Marian prayer is from Egypt." *Aleteia,* April 29, 2017. https://aleteia.org/2017/04/29/the-oldest-known-marian-prayer-is-from-egypt/.

Marshall, Taylor. "The Mysterious Relics of St. Anne." *Taylor Marshall* (blog) July 26, 2013. http://taylormarshall.com/2013/07/the-mysterious-relics-of-saint-anne.html.